EDUCATION IN TRANSITION
WHAT ROLE FOR RESEARCH?

a collection of papers
to mark the 60th Anniversary
of the founding
of
The Scottish Council for Research in Education

edited by
Sally Brown
and
Rosemary Wake

The Scottish Council for Research in Education

SCRE Publication Number 102

The views expressed in these papers are those of the authors and do not necessarily reflect those of the Council.

ISBN 0 947833 28 5

Printed and bound in Great Britain for The Scottish Council for Research in Education by Polyprint, 48 Pleasance, Edinburgh EH8 9TJ.

CONTENTS

		Page
1	*The Researchers of Scottish Education* Sally Brown, The Scottish Council for Research in Education	1
2	*The Contribution of Research to Education* John Nisbet, University of Aberdeen	14
3	*Persistence and Change in Teacher Education* Gordon Kirk, Moray House College of Education	25
4	*Research and Change in the Education of Girls* *and Women in Scotland* Margaret Sutherland, Emeritus Professor of Education, University of Leeds	35
5	*Has Schooling a Future?* David Hamilton, University of Glasgow	47
6	*Vocationalism and Economic Recovery:* *the case against witchcraft* Ian Stronach, University of East Anglia	55
7	*Research about Parents in Education* Alastair Macbeth, University of Glasgow	71
8	*Resource-based Teaching: the new pedagogy?* Eric Drever, University of Stirling	86
9	*Radical Pedagogy for Conservative Schooling? 14-18 in Scotland* David Hartley, University of Dundee	97
10	*Going with the Grain: youth training in transition* David Raffe, University of Edinburgh	110
11	*The Transition from Beginning Student-Teacher* *to Fluent Classroom Teacher* Donald McIntyre, University of Oxford	124
12	*Transitions and Early Education* Margaret M. Clark, Emeritus Professor of Education, University of Birmingham	142
13	*The Role of Research?* Sally Brown, The Scottish Council for Research in Education	153

Acronyms

CAST	—	Curriculum Advice and Support Team
CCC	—	Consultative Committee on the Curriculum (now the Scottish Consultative Council on the Curriculum)
CNAA	—	Council for National Academic Awards
CPVE	—	Certificate of Pre-Vocational Education
CHES	—	Child Health and Education Study
CBI	—	Confederation of British Industries
CSS	—	Contemporary Social Studies
DES	—	Department of Education and Science
DHSS	—	Department of Health and Social Security
EIS	—	Educational Institute of Scotland
FEU	—	Further Education Unit
GTC	—	General Teaching Council
MSC	—	Manpower Services Commission (now the Training Agency)
NEDO	—	National Economic Development Office
PSD	—	Personal and Social Development
SCCC	—	Scottish Consultative Council on the Curriculum
SCOSDE	—	Scottish Committee for Staff Development in Education
SCOTVEC	—	Scottish Vocational Education Council
SCRE	—	Scottish Council for Research in Education
SEB	—	Scottish Examination Board
SED	—	Scottish Education Department
SSRC	—	Social Science Research Council (now the Economic and Social Research Council)
SSTA	—	Scottish Secondary Teachers' Association
STEAC	—	Scottish Tertiary Education Advisory Council
SVS	—	Social and Vocational Skills
SYPS	—	Scottish Young Peoples Survey
TVEI	—	Technical and Vocational Education Initiative
UGC	—	Universty Grants Committee
YOP	—	Youth Opportunities Programme
YTS	—	Youth Training Scheme

1

The Researchers of Scottish Education

Sally Brown

Introduction

In the Jubilee year of the Scottish Council for Research in Education (SCRE) a great deal has been made of the role of educational practitioners in its establishment back in 1928. Quite rightly the efforts of teachers' unions and directors of education have been applauded. Decisions in those early days have been highly influential in sustaining the Council's activities so that our major emphasis is still on applied research which is designed to play a supportive role in Scottish education. And those activities have been made possible over the years by funding from different groups of educational policy makers.

There is, however, another group, apart from practitioners and policy makers, which has played a major part in the development of SCRE: the research community. Without the help of that community we would have sacrificed critical dialogue, been short of research training, had much more difficulty in maintaining research standards, been exposed to far fewer new ideas, experienced substantially less development in methodology and been in greater danger of ideological rhetoric gaining ascendancy over rational analysis.

The Council decided, therefore, that it would be appropriate in 1988, its Jubilee year, to publish a collection of papers by educational researchers in Scotland, and Scots undertaking such work elsewhere. We invited a small number of such people to make a contribution around the loose theme of *Education in Transition*. All the authors were given a free hand and we have been parsimonious in our editing. As a result, we have to say that as editors we do not agree with all of the views expressed, nor are these views necessarily those of the Council. But we have found all the contributions both absorbing and stimulating.

The theme can be interpreted, of course, as being concerned with changes in educational systems, or with transition points within systems (such as the transition from primary to secondary education). The authors were left to choose their own interpretation of transition and the particular topic they would address. They were requested, however, to take a research perspective on their chosen issue. How they did that was for them to decide: it might take the form of the text being a report or review of research; they could reflect on the contribution of research to policy or practice; or they might look forward to research which would inform or facilitate educational change in the future.

Such freedom of choice does not lead to a coherent structure of inter-related contributions. What it does is to provide an opportunity for a set of eminent individual researchers to write about the issues which have particular salience for their current thinking about education.

Unfortunately, we could not invite all of the talented researchers in Scottish education to contribute. This is but a small sample. It does indicate, however, the broad spread of educational matters which currently are the focus of attention and it identifies a number of different perspectives on research. These perspectives on research are considered in Chapter 13. The rest of this chapter provides an outline of what is to be found in the book, and a brief introduction to each of the researchers.

The ordering of the chapters in this book is related loosely to the kind of 'transition' to which each author has directed his or her attention. So, for example, in the first few chapters the authors have been concerned with how particular facets of education have changed over relatively long periods of time: John Nisbet looks at changes in educational research itself during the sixty years since SCRE was founded; Gordon Kirk takes us through a century of changes in the professional preparation of teachers; and Margaret Sutherland charts the changes in education for women since the end of the second world war. David Hamilton takes the reader back even further to the twelfth century; the purpose of his analysis is explicitly to try to make sense of today's attempts by government to reform schooling.

Making sense, in different ways, of current reforms is also the focus for Ian Stronach (who addresses vocationalism), Alastair Macbeth (who looks at the role of parents in schooling), Eric Drever (whose concern is resource-based teaching), David Hartley (who examines new curricular provision) and David Raffe (whose interest is new training schemes for young people).

The last of these is additionally concerned with transition in the sense of change for the individual young person; in this case, that related to moving on from school to labour market. Donald McIntyre and Margaret Clark also focus on change for the individual: from student-teacher to classroom teacher, and from pre-school to primary school education respectively.

John Nisbet

In any account of educational research in Scotland, or of SCRE itself, John Nisbet would have a central place. His leadership of the research community has become a legend. Eminence and scholarship is obvious, whether one looks at his position as Professor at the University of Aberdeen, his role with others in founding the British Educational Research Association, his continual support for the Scottish Educational Research Association, his international reputation for research and teaching, his tireless encouragement for those new to research, his intrepid defence of research against hostile forces, his amazingly clear and thorough writing about education, or the regard in which he is held by anyone who has ever been his student. His connections with SCRE are particularly close. He chaired the Council from 1975 to 1978, and we greatly value the fact that he has the Fellowship of SCRE which is awarded for a prolonged and outstanding contribution to educational research.

The aspect of 'transition' on which John chooses to focus in Chapter 2 is the change in educational research itself. In comparing research in the circumstances in which SCRE was set up in 1928 with that of the present day, however, the reader is left wondering if there has been as much change as one might expect. John argues persuasively that current preferences for teachers' involvement in classroom action research are strikingly close to William Boyd's ideas in the years leading up to the establishment of SCRE. Furthermore, the 'solution of problems' emphasis in the 1920s has its parallel in the Rothschild Report's customer-contractor formula of the 1970s.

Perhaps the most telling aspect of this chapter is the analysis of the conditions under which research makes a contribution, direct or indirect, to policy and practice. Pressure for relevance, for example, may actually constrain the value of what research has to offer policy makers and practitioners. The dangers of short-term projects, which simply address those questions seen by policy makers as relevant to their immediate needs, are outlined. If there are no resources or time to scrutinise the assumptions which underpin existing policy and practice, then important issues will be neglected as will the opportunities 'to awaken new expectations of what might be possible'. John suggests that 'in the long term the best hope for research may rest with . . . the teachers'. Others might go further and say 'will rest'; but John has some cautions for them on the pitfalls of that road. He is firm that 'we must recognise [that there are] different styles of research, and different ways in which it may contribute to education'. Whatever the style, however, excessive control from the centre will inhibit the flowering of research.

Gordon Kirk

Gordon Kirk, Principal of Moray House College of Education, has been Chairman of SCRE since 1984. He has led the Council through difficult times for research and has been unfailingly creative and supportive (of both the Board of Management and the staff of SCRE) in the decision-making in which he has been a central figure. He is unafraid of standing up to anyone, whether the established academic community, central government or the teaching profession. Decisions, he knows, will always be unpopular with some sector of the education community, but it is to his great credit that he evaluates himself as keenly as he does his opponents. His un-failing robustness in debate, in conjunction with irrepressible good humour, have made him a strong chairman, and SCRE has much to thank him for.

Appropriately, Gordon has chosen to interpret 'transition' in terms of the changes which Scotland has seen in the professional preparation of teachers. His text in Chapter 3 concentrates on four facets of these changes. First, he discusses the evolution from a practical training of teachers (avoiding 'heavy academic orientation'), through the notion of 'BEd degrees controlled by the universities', to an autonomous BEd for primary teachers from Scottish colleges of education with CNAA validation. His second concern focuses on the increasing involvement of practising teachers in the process of teacher education. He charts developments prior to the establishment of the General Teaching Council and that Council's growth of influence on teacher training. The colleges' new conceptions of the nature and purposes of student-teachers' school experiences, the increasing role of teachers in selection of students and college courses, and the importance in the eyes of official bodies (such as SED and CNAA) of colleges' partnership with teachers, have all led to greater influence and responsibility for practitioners in programmes of professional training. Gordon's third theme charts the patterns of SED control of teacher education. His thesis suggests while there was some weakening of this control after the establishment of the General Teaching Council in 1965, 'since the late '70s, that control has been vigorously reasserted' and is now 'even more prescriptive and intrusive'. Finally, he addresses the institutional context of teacher education and rehearses the history and arguments for specialist colleges for teacher education.

In considering research, Gordon concludes that apart from 'its role in connection with the increased involvement of the profession in teacher education . . . research has played no great part in the developments described'. If he is right, then that is a salutary jolt for educational researchers. If research is about extending knowledge, then can it have been largely irrelevant to the evolution of teacher education?

Margaret Sutherland

Margaret Sutherland is an exceptional educationalist. That statement is confirmed by the statistics given in her own contribution to this book: as a Professor at the University of Leeds she was one of the tiny proportion (2.8 per cent) of women among those at professorial level in universities in England. Had she remained in Scotland, her task would have been even more difficult: here the proportion is only 2.4 per cent. Margaret has been an inspiration to many academic women who have seen her maintain extraordinarily high standards of work in the face of traditional attitudes, which may now be improving (see her chapter) but did nothing to ease *her* career path. We are particularly grateful that despite much of her work being carried out in Northern Ireland and the north of England, she has consistently kept contact with Scotland, and done much as a model for, and encouragement to, young women researchers here. SCRE awarded her, and Margaret Clark, its Fellowship in 1988. On the occasion of her Fellowship address she showed us that her excellence is apparent not only in her writing, but also in her remarkable fluency of oral presentation.

The sense in which Margaret interprets 'transition' in Chapter 4 is concerned with changes in the education of women since the Second World War. She documents these changes and makes international comparisons from which she gains the impression that 'the situation of girls in Scotland . . . does not differ much from the situation in other European or "developed" countries'. This situation displays women's improved access to education and standards of attainment, together with some changes in attitude. But there are still profound gender differences at the highest levels of education, despite the evidence at the lower levels of women's very considerable potential.

Margaret offers the reader a meticulous outline of research on gender differences: national surveys, longitudinal studies and the most recent work on school leavers. But she reminds us that in Scotland we lack research which focuses on classroom interaction, young people's classroom behaviour, teacher attitudes and school organisation — all of which have profound effects on the 'differentiation of role and expectations of future studies and employment'. Although she warns of the possible defects of small-scale, idiosyncratic 'illuminative' research, she points to the potential richness of the relatively unknown MEd theses. In her chapter she persuasively and eloquently presents the argument for the importance of having small-scale work, in conjunction with large-scale systematic monitoring, document analysis and carefully designed qualitative studies. This, she argues, can enable us better to understand the educational opportunities which are offered to women.

David Hamilton
David Hamilton is an international figure in educational research,

working in the Department of Education at Glasgow University. From the days when he and Malcolm Parlett coined the phrase 'illuminative evaluation', he has had world-wide respect for his philosophical approach to educational matters. Not only has he made us think more deeply about our educational research and practice, he also has initiated a plethora of new ways of approaching issues which are of major practical importance. He provides a splendid example of the lateral thinker who adopts a disciplined approach to the application of theory to practice.

In Chapter 5 he reflects 'transition' in the context of two of his research interests: 'making sense of contemporary changes within schooling' and appreciating 'the ways in which, through the ages, schooling has been linked to other social institutions such as the family, the church, the state and the labour market'. He uses historical research to illuminate and understand current educational issues and, in particular, what he refers to as the proposals tabled for 'a fundamental restructuring of schooling'.

David poses the questions of whether these proposals signal a time of transition or a time of crisis, innovation or upheaval, a centralising initiative or a redistribution of power. He takes us from the origins of schooling in the twelfth century, where the Church's purposes for cathedral schools was 'the enforcement rather than the interpretation of canon law' through the sixteenth century nation state when 'populations were to be converted, en masse, to a new set of social, economic and moral principles'. His claim that for the next 450 years (including 1928 when SCRE was formed) schooling was conceived of as 'social regulation *cum* social transformation', is followed by a penetrating question: are the apparently contradictory elements of the 1988 reforms, the weakening of state control by 'opting out' of schools and its strengthening by a national curriculum, a reflection of 'an uneasy merger of individual politicians' wish lists' or evidence of a very 'sophisticated model of political devolution'? The evidence he offers suggests the former.

Ian Stronach

It is several years since Ian Stronach left Scotland to go and work at the University of East Anglia. His earlier research and writing at the Scottish Vocational Preparation Unit, at Jordanhill College of Education in Glasgow, earned him a considerable reputation as an analyst of policy and practice. While we now see less of him in Scotland than we might wish, reports still reach us from academics and postgraduate students south of the border, that his contribution to theory and research is exceptional. He says his heart is still in the west of Scotland; we look forward to his return one day.

In Chapter 6, 'transition' is set in vocationalism and Ian focuses on the personal transformation which is called for in individual young people in pursuit of the country's general economic recovery. The chapter is itself the research analysis and it seeks first to unpack the so-called 'rationality' which links the education and training of the individual to broad economic goals. In a powerful and demanding way it examines the nature of, and case for, vocational education presented in the 1986 Government White Paper on Education and Training. Ian scrutinises what he sees as the alarming simplicity of the proposed solutions to economic problems, ie 'good education training = higher worker productivity = economic success'.

The most striking facet of the analysis is the analogy he draws between vocationalism and ritual. Vocational initiatives have a persuasiveness, part of which, Ian argues, is ritualistic. He takes us through the identification of economic decline as something for which the inadequacies in training and motivation of young people are blamed, the responsibility which is placed on those young people for economic recovery, the emergence of work as the 'sacred centre' and the vocational initiatives which are offered as a response, rather than a solution, to the 'problem'. The relationship of these (and other) characteristics of vocationalism with those of ritual are illuminated. In particular, the analysis concludes that vocational initiatives, like rituals, flow from 'a need to reassure the powerful'. Rationales for such initiatives are invariably couched in terms of progress to economic prosperity and a 'better' life for young people. What this chapter does, is to challenge the reader to see such activity as, in part, a ritual which satisfies the powerful among the adult population that a government response to the 'problem' is in hand; 'it is the performance that is important, and the audience [the powerful] rather than the actors [young people] or the plot'. Ian distinguishes his arguments which relate to ritual, from the Marxist ideological critiques which provide explanations in terms of 'mystification and manipulation of the young'. While the Marxist believes 'they [those in power] are clever and . . . out to deceive us', the ritual contends 'they are stupid . . . and out to deceive themselves'.

Alastair Macbeth
In the last decade or so, Alastair Macbeth of Glasgow University has been seen as someone in the forefront of research into matters which are profoundly important to the interface between pupils' institutional experiences and all of their other life. His expertise is constantly in demand to fuel the debates in Scotland on schools' councils, parental choice of schools and, now, school boards. His knowledge of the field is prodigious as is his willingness to share it with the rest of us and his ability

to write about difficult concepts succinctly and with great clarity. It takes a particularly high quality of researcher to remain, as he does, serene and industrious in an area of study which is both difficult and a political minefield.

Alastair takes the opportunity in Chapter 7 to consider a 'transition' in education which he describes by saying 'The spotlight is being turned on parents'. He reminds us how important parents are in education and that '85 per cent of a child's waking (and therefore learning) life . . . is spent *out* of school'. Despite this, almost all our emphasis in educational research in Scotland has been directed on institutional provision with virtually nothing on home learning or community learning. In particular, he is concerned that 'the place of parents in education has been insufficiently researched'.

Chapter 7 is not, however, just a wringing of hands about the inadequacy of our attempts to understand the effects of, and interactions among, the different factors inside and outside school which influence children's learning. On the contrary, Alastair provides a practical and specific agenda for research. He includes proposals for work on parental perceptions of education, document analysis, the monitoring of changes (such as school boards) introduced by legislation, communication between parents and schools, the relationship between certain pupil characteristics (performance in school, behaviour, truancy) and home background variables, parental access to records and reports on their children, the roles of associations involving parents, the micropolitics of home-school relations, homework, home learning, and the relative importance of the various influences on what children learn. This surely provides an excellent outline for a programme of interlinking research projects. It is the antithesis of, and potentially of far greater value than, the kinds of short-term highly focused projects currently favoured by funding bodies but cautioned against by John Nisbet in Chapter 2.

Eric Drever
Eric Drever is the author of Chapter 8. His research into teaching and assessment at the University of Stirling has been well-known since the early seventies. Most, but not all, of that work has been associated in some way with science education, and it has gained him considerable recognition not only from other researchers but also from the teachers, HM Inspectors and local authority advisers whose daily bread is science in schools. He combines research, initial-teacher training and in-service work with a quiet flair and remarkable competence which is respected in many corners of Scottish education. His eye is always on the practical application of research findings, and on providing support for teachers by

helping them better to understand the educational scenarios in which they find themselves.

The focus of Eric Drever's contribution is research concerned with resource-based teaching. 'Transition' in this chapter, therefore, is associated with the change in pedagogy which accompanies a trend to individualised or resource-based learning. Unlike reforms such as comprehensivisation, raising of the school leaving age or certification for all, developments in teaching methods have not occupied the front line in official documents. It could be argued, of course, that such developments have arisen from the documents' apparent emphasis on change towards skills to replace content, process instead of product, and pupil-centred as opposed to teacher-led education. Eric's belief, however, is that the most powerful thrust for resource-based teaching, for the fourteen to sixteen age group in Scotland, has been the implication in the new Standard Grade programme in the Scottish Certificate of Education that classes be mixed ability with the young people working on material at a variety of levels.

A role for research in this pedagogical transition is illustrated with a report of a particular empirical investigation of a resource-based development: *Choice Chemistry*. The account provides both a down-to-earth picture of what has been implemented, and a studied analysis of what is going on in resource-based classrooms and how that compares with more traditional pedagogic approaches. The value of research of this kind is that it is directed at the practitioner, but does not presume to make the practical decisions about implementation. It provides a range of findings from the very positive attitudes which many pupils have to resource-based teaching, through the dangers of objectives-based systems which encourage the 'do it, check it, forget it' syndrome rather than a coherent body of learning, to the almost total lack of evidence for the improvement of cognitive learning in these contexts when compared with traditional settings. Research of this kind does not provide a judgmental tick (or cross), but it offers valuable information which practitioners can use in deciding what action to take.

David Hartley

It is always particularly pleasing to have a contribution from a researcher who is also a member of the Council, in this case representing the Scottish Universities Council for Studies in Education. David Hartley of Dundee University is well-known for his thoughtful and radical analyses of contemporary educational matters; he is less well-known for the considerate and constructive advice he has given to the Council during his time there.

In Chapter 9, David interprets research as a critical analysis of educational developments directed at what he sees as 'an emerging social category in educational discourse: "young people", normally of less-than-average ability and aged between 14 and 18'. The 'transition' he senses is one in which 'an emerging institutional educational structure for "young people" of this type . . . would do much to undermine the ideal that [is] the comprehensive . . . school'. He uses the Standard Grade course *Social and Vocational Skills* for 14 to 16 year olds, and the *Personal and Social Development* in the 16+ programme to illustrate what he sees as 'the curricular catalysts of this new provision'.

The analysis takes the reader nicely through the apparently urgent moves to make explicit what was previously regarded as the hidden curriculum, and so to inculcate 'right attitudes'. David argues the case that there has been a distinctive move towards an association of courses in schools (SVS) and in further education colleges (PSD) and that this relatively integrated approach is providing a radical pedagogy; that pedagogy, however, delivers an essentially conservative notion of schooling. By that he means schooling which is specifically targeted at low-achievers, provides the social and communication skills needed by industry when employment is available, and fosters the self-sufficiency necessary for the 'the young unemployed worker to cope with the [considerable] adversity he [or she] faces'. This emphasis on service for the economy may, he suggests, 'render the individual passive in the face of . . . adversity' if he or she is exposed to such education from 14 to 18. And by 'adversity' he seems mostly to mean unemployment.

David Raffe

The Centre for Educational Sociology at the University of Edinburgh has an international reputation for high quality research. A substantial proportion of that research has been carried out by David Raffe. Although he is the first to acknowledge the importance of team work, as an individual he is regarded as in the highest rank of researchers in Scotland. As well as considerable technical competence, particularly in the areas of survey design and analysis, his ability to communicate about research, whether by writing or speaking, is much admired. At conferences, his relaxed, down-to-earth, clear and interesting presentations of what otherwise may appear dull and complicated numerical analyses, are a model for other researchers to follow.

In Chapter 10 David's focus is on 'transition' in two senses: the transition of young people from school to the labour market, and the transition of the Government's Youth Opportunities Programme (YOP) to the Youth Training Scheme (YTS) in its evolving forms. He illustrates in a striking way how empirical research using a large-scale survey can illuminate not just the overall effects of, and young people's reactions to, these government schemes, but also the covert factors which determine whether the schemes will provide skills which young people can 'sell' to the wider labour market or will simply train them for the needs of the YTS employer.

This chapter demonstrates how regular surveys of school leavers, together with longitudinal studies of school year groups, can generate the knowledge needed to understand the nature and effects of these schemes. David notes the modest increases in the proportion of each cohort of leavers going onto YTS in comparison with YOP, and its ability to recruit more of the middle-range ('O' grades) achievers. But although YTS seems to be a better route to employment than does an initial period of unemployment, its training potential seems to have little advantage for those who have the choice of going straight into employment from school. His analysis goes on to show that the main achievement of YTS is to provide opportunities for employment, but only with those employers who are in the scheme. 'It seems to have conformed to a British pattern of training for the internal labour market and for firms' own needs . . . but the general marketability of YTS training in the external labour market is yet to be demonstrated'. Because his research approach is rigorous, and his arguments are clear and open, substantial credence can be attached to his conclusions. He suggests that the reason for the failure of YTS to develop a 'system whose products are highly marketable in the external labour market' is that employers are reluctant to give weight to general vocational qualifications; they prefer to train for their own immediate needs. From him that is a persuasive statement; as a personal (and probably political) view of others, it would be less so.

Donald McIntyre

Chapter 11 is written by Donald McIntyre who was a major force in educational research in Scotland for two decades. He spent most of this time at the University of Stirling where his research on teaching and teacher-education earned him a national and international reputation. Those who have worked closely with him over the years, and I am one of them, cannot speak highly enough of his intellect, support for other researchers, rigour in research and vast knowledge of educational ideas and research methods. It was Scotland's loss and the University of Oxford's gain, when this extraordinarily creative man moved south. Many of his colleagues have felt, however, that more of his work should have been published, so that the wider world can have access to the ideas which co-workers already value so highly. It is with particular pleasure, therefore, that we include a contribution from him in this book.

The aspect of 'transition' on which Donald focuses is that of the student-teacher developing into a fluent classroom teacher. Teacher-educators may have clear plans for this, but several factors have a profound effect on whether the *actual* learning proceeds according to those plans. The understandings which students bring to their initial training, from years of contact with their own teachers, will only slowly be modified. Their own agendas for their training may be different from those of the teacher-educators. And in the more emotional areas, students' needs to reduce stress, or unrealistic over-optimism, may ensure that they make sense of, and react to, their experiences in very personal ways. Initial training offers enormous social complexity, different messages and diversity of practice. They may be asked to communicate to different people, such as supervising teachers and college tutors, in different ways about different things at different levels according to the other person's priorities for, say, concrete practical details or theoretical matters. When they reach the end of their initial training, beginning-teachers are still in an important period of their learning.

Donald draws our attention to the crucial importance of research into the learning of beginning-teachers. He reviews the substantial body of competent work which has already been carried out in this area, much of it in North America. Some of this research has addressed directly the transition from student-teacher to experienced teacher, but other studies (which, he argues, are equally important for the interpretation of data on student-teachers) focus instead on the nature of experienced teachers' expertise. His critique of this body of work provides us with a powerful agenda for future research in teacher-education.

Margaret Clark

In Margaret Clark, Scotland has once more produced a researcher who has put her considerable talents at the disposal of practical educational matters. Her reputation in early education and the study of reading is international. By accepting a chair at the University of Birmingham she became yet another export, and further evidence of what Michael Shea (1988) was referring to when he recently said 'The MacMafia is alive and well and operating very smoothly down here'. That SCRE has been continually impressed by her work must be evident from the award of the Council's Fellowship to her, and to Margaret Sutherland, in this our Jubilee year. The contribution which Margaret Clark's research has made to our understanding of crucial aspects of education has been immense.

Margaret's essay (Chapter 12) takes us through the earliest transitions in the child's educational career. It marries much practical information with research findings. Even at the stage of transition from preschool education, or the home, to primary school, the distinctions between the Scottish and English systems are apparent. For example, the local authorities in Scotland have relatively uniform policies on age of entry to the primary reception class in contrast with the variation among the English authorities. Unfortunately, changes in these entry ages over the past few years have led, in some cases, to primary teachers having responsibility for children who are younger than those for whom they are trained. Because the plans of the early 1970s for expansion of preschool provision were never implemented, many people have assumed there has been no increase in the numbers of children attending nursery classes or schools. In fact, these numbers have increased dramatically, but to vastly different extents in different authorities.

In reviewing the research literature, Margaret points to some gaps such as a lack of 'evidence on observational studies of children from ethnic minorities in their homes at the preschool stage'. There is, however, much to be learned from the body of knowledge which research has helped to accumulate. She points to the work which has been done on children who have language difficulties or other special educational needs on entry, the problems such needs pose for teachers, the curriculum and its progression for both those who have and those who have not had preschool education, the organisation of preschool education, the role of parents in the transition and the potential of young children which can so easily be crushed. Policy makers concerned with raising standards would do well to heed her conclusions, based on sound evidence, about 'the danger that too narrow a programme and formal testing of young children, may altogether confirm teachers in their belief in limited expectations of children', and that the 'free ethos, choice and better adult-child ratio in preschools has potential for development of the children's language, ability to concentrate, for collaboration between peers and as a foundation for literacy and numeracy'.

In conclusion

These contributions have engendered in us an awareness of the multiplicity of changing facets of education. They also reiterate the importance of research to the understanding of educational matters by professionals and others alike. As an institute devoted to educational research, we have reason to celebrate authors of these chapters and all of our other colleagues in the institutions which share our commitment to extending knowledge.

Reference
SHEA, M (1988) 'Power or influence?' *The Scotsman,* 24 September 1988

2

The Contribution of Research to Education

John Nisbet

Our expectations of what research can do are shaped by analogies with other disciplines. But many of these analogies are misleading. Research in medicine is popularly seen as the discovery of new treatments which control disease and suffering. In pure science, experiments refine theories and establish underlying laws and principles. In agriculture, research has been so successful (in developed countries) that there are now problems of surplus and a diminished labour force. Some educational researchers have aspired to aims such as these: an initial teaching alphabet to eliminate difficulty in learning to read; psychological experiments to establish laws of learning; or educational technology which would make teachers unnecessary. But they have not succeeded — not yet, at least. A different analogy allots a subordinate role to research, as for example in architecture, where research on materials may be helpful to ensure that buildings do not collapse but the prime task of the architect is to create an environment, and in this task people's preferences and fashion, not research, are dominant considerations. The cynic may liken educational research to literary criticism or art, where changing fashions reign supreme, or to politics where the limited function of research is to strengthen the hands of those who seek power and wish to persuade. If we must have an analogy, I suggest comparing education to cheese, which has many varieties with different qualities. Research on cheese is complicated by the plurality of tastes and values. (De Gaulle is said to have asked, in frustration: 'How can one govern a country that has 240 different kinds of cheese?')

Direct and indirect contributions of research
Wake's (1988) research on the origins of SCRE illustrates the founders' reliance on the analogy with research in industry and applied science. In 1917, a Scottish Education Reform Committee argued the case for educational research on this basis:

> All the considerations which have led to a general recognition of the importance of scientific research as an aid to industry apply with equal force to education. . . . What is wanted to raise the level of efficiency in school work is the . . . constant examination of existing practice by scientific methods. . . . (quoted by Wake).

14

The Reform Committee's report led the Educational Institute of Scotland to set up a Research in Education Committee in 1919, which implemented a decade of practical research activities throughout Scotland; and this in turn laid the basis for the establishment of the Council in 1928.

An interesting aspect of these far-off events is that they anticipate questions which are still at issue today. Can research 'raise the level of efficiency in school work'? What kind of research is most likely to contribute towards this aim? The Reform Committee suggested a distinction between 'theoretical' research, 'which industrial experience shows to have the highest value in suggesting new ideas', and 'practical' research, 'directed to the solution of definite problems in educational practice' (quotations from Wake). Theoretical research could best be done in universities and colleges; practical research should be tackled by inspectors and teachers. The activities of the EIS Research Committee which followed were designed to involve teachers directly in research, either through Local Research Committees or in national 'experiments'. These experiments were co-ordinated by William Boyd of Glasgow University (who did not accept the 'theoretical research' role of universities), and were orchestrated through the columns of the *Scottish Educational Journal*. Topics investigated included teaching spelling, marking composition, speeding handwriting and 'getting rid of lumber' in the curriculum. Though the argument of Wake's article is that the underlying motive in all this was to use research to strengthen the teacher's claim to professional status, the precise form of this initiative is an anticipation, hitherto unrecognised, of the teacher-as-researcher movement of the 1970s.

The emphasis on practical research — the 'solution of problems' — can also be viewed as an anticipation of the customer-contractor formula of the 1971 Rothschild Report. The expectation that practical research will solve problems in education derives from analogy with other fields of activity like engineering or medicine, and it is the cause of some disillusion when research fails to resolve important educational controversies. Practical research has made a significant direct contribution to educational policy and practice, but only in non-controversial areas where there is consensus on values. In controversial areas, the influence of research is indirect and longer-term, through analysis, new interpretations and new concepts accumulating over time to influence the climate of opinion — not so much offering solutions to problems but rather defining the problem to which solutions must be sought:

> The impact of research is essentially in determining what kinds of questions and evidence are seen as important, and how they are seen — how practitioners

and researchers (and administrators and policy-makers) structure their perceptions of their work. In this way, research creates an agenda of concern.

(Broadfoot *and* Nisbet, 1981)

Fortunately there are plenty of examples where research has made a direct contribution to policy and practice: the education of children with special needs (especially the deaf), the design of textbooks (especially for beginning readers), remedial education (especially screening and diagnostic work), learning a second language, and so on. What they have in common is that they are all relatively non-controversial areas, and since there is a consensus on values, research findings are readily incorporated into policy or action. In controversial areas, when basic assumptions are challenged (even in the 'agreed' topics listed above), then research findings tend to be treated merely as if they came from one more pressure group (and they are readily taken up by groups whose arguments are supported by the findings). The example of selection for secondary education illustrates the point. When the task was to decide which was the most efficient combination of tests for the 11 plus, research was used to improve the reliability and validity of the selection procedure, and did it very well. But when the ground shifted to the different question of whether selection at 11 plus was itself a 'correct' policy, then the function of research changed dramatically, being concerned primarily with identifying weaknesses in the selection policy and with clarifying issues. This is the indirect, long-term function of research, creating the context within which controversial issues are tackled. In this long-term process, what happens is that new concepts or theories are advanced, and are gradually absorbed into popular discussion until they become a new climate of opinion. This indirect influence has been stressed by many of those who have written about the impact of research. Weiss (1977) described it as 'a gradual accumulation of research results which can lead to far-reaching changes in the way people and governments address their problems'; Getzels (1973) wrote of 'a cumulative altering of conceptions of human behaviour'; Cronbach and Suppes (1969) described it as the emergence of 'a prevailing view'; and Taylor (1973) called it a process of 'sensitising' public opinion.

There have been many changes in education since 1928 when SCRE was founded: comprehensive education, the growth of continuing education and the massive increase in numbers in further and higher education, changes in the examination system, new developments in method and curriculum, open plan schools, computers in education, new management structures, and changes in the climate and personal relationships in schools. Few would claim that these changes occurred because of rational planning based on research. McPherson and Raab

(1988) argue that changes in policy reflect the favoured ideas of the individuals who temporarily hold positions of power in the educational system. But the diffusion of research findings in the form of 'ideas in good currency' (Schon, 1971) influenced these individuals and also helped to establish the basis for acceptance of their views. (A cynical view is that change in education occurs because the old die off and are replaced by younger people who grew up with a different set of assumptions, which they in turn proceed to build into a new orthodoxy.) In the period 1965-85, possibly the four publications most influential on policy in Scottish education were the Primary Memorandum of 1965 (SED), the Munn Report (SED) and the Dunning Report (SED) of 1977, and the Action Plan of 1983 (SED). These owed little to the direct influence of research, with the possible exception of Dunning. But the Primary Memorandum and Munn and Dunning were very much affected by the climate of opinion which resulted from the indirect influence of research.

The distinction between the direct and indirect contributions of research to education can be expressed in terms of two contrasting functions of educational research, the *instrumental* and the *enlightenment* functions. There is a strong case for viewing the function of research in education as primarily *instrumental*: its task is to help people achieve what they (and not the researchers) want to achieve. Most people acknowledge that their aspirations may not be realisable exactly in the way they would like, and are willing to look to research to identify effective means of achieving their aims and avoiding unintended or unforeseen consequences. In contrast, the *enlightenment* function of research in the social sciences is concerned with changing people's perceptions, influencing their aspirations, questioning assumptions and offering new insights. The term 'enlightenment' may be criticised as arrogant: even more emotive are the terms 'exploitative' and 'emancipatory', used by Giddens (1982) to contrast the use of social science to extend the power of management and its use to strengthen the autonomy of the individual. The issue here is whether the function of research is to aid the managers or to challenge them, whether the aim of research is to improve the smooth running of the system or to restructure and reform it. Or, of course, whether it can do both.

The pressure for relevance

Throughout its existence, SCRE has had to take account of the expectation that its research would make a direct contribution to the problems of the day. Depending on external funding, it was under pressure from the start to demonstrate the relevance of research to the concerns of those who provided its income. The Council set out to be of value to teachers, and many of its early publications reflect this emphasis, especially for the primary school: *Studies in Arithmetic* (SCRE, 1939 and 1941), *Studies in Reading* (SCRE, 1948 and 1950), *Achievement Tests in the Primary School* (MacGregor, 1934), *Addition and Subtraction Facts and Processes* (SCRE, 1949), *The Writing of Arabic Numerals* (Wright, 1952), *Studies in Spelling* (SCRE, 1961), *Selection for Secondary Education* (McClelland, 1942). Because almost all the work was done by unpaid volunteers, SCRE was also able to publish a series of academic studies, in psychology and history, which won it an international reputation among researchers. But it was the practical style of inquiry which won support for SCRE and for educational research at the time when it needed support, and strengthened the case for increased research funding. The early work was done on a shoestring: in 1960, after 30 years' operation, the total annual budget of SCRE was £8,338. The move to full-time staff in the 1970s instead of committees of volunteers required a new source of funds, and this came from the Scottish Education Department: in 1978, at its peak, the budget was £316,000, of which £135,000 came from SED. The pressure for relevance increased with greater dependence on central funding. The 1988 list of current publications continues to demonstrate the relevant contribution which research can make directly to educational problems in the system: *Discipline in School* (Johnstone *and* Munn, 1987), *Assessing Modules* (Black, Hall *and* Yates, 1987), *Science and Computers in Primary Education* (Adams, 1985), *Criterion-Referenced Assessment in the Classroom* (Black *and* Dockrell, 1984), an evaluation of community schools, a series of briefing papers 'of interest to practitioners', a new series of Practitioner Mini Papers, and so on.

The danger inherent in the concept of 'relevance' is that relevance is liable to mean 'within the framework of existing policy, or compatible with existing practice'. There is then a risk that only those ideas will be considered which can be incorporated within the present system as it is and which leave prejudices unchallenged — resulting in 'innovation without change'. No one is suggesting that research should be irrelevant. But the definition of relevance has to be drawn widely, to ensure that important issues are not excluded from the agenda, to give alternative viewpoints fair consideration, and even to awaken new expectations of what might be possible. Otherwise, research may be limited to miniscule inquiry, resulting in only marginal change; it would be preoccupied with short-term studies, and with product rather than process; and it could have a reactionary influence:

> By reinforcing the framework of thought which identifies certain aspects as 'problems', legitimating their priority in the agenda of concern, . . . (research could have) a stabilising effect which discourages alternative perspectives.
>
> (Broadfoot *and* Nisbet, 1981)

In general, those who administer funds for research in education have recognised that it is no use having a separate research organisation if it is too closely under control. Consequently, there is provision for supporting, 'at a modest level, important research ideas from the field' (SERA, 1987). However, official listing of priority topics has been published since 1986. The present list includes college/industry liaison, opportunities for mature students (including PICKUP and other MSC initiatives), differentiation of learning and teaching in primary schools, evaluation of a recruitment scheme for engineering and technology, and drug education.

The Winter 1987 Newsletter of the Scottish Educational Research Association carried a series of short articles on the current state of educational research in Scotland. (The list quoted above was taken from the Scottish Education Department's contribution to the series.) One theme which recurs in several of the articles is concern at increasing centralisation of research:

> . . . the general move away from a system which encouraged the Colleges to identify and promote their research priorities. . . . What resulted was undoubtedly good: the best projects were funded and the colleges were very much in control of the direction of their research enterprise. Such a system has now been replaced by a structure which directs SED funds more emphatically towards research in areas of major concern to the Department. (Colleges of Education)

> . . . almost without exception policy-orientated research, and usually . . . short-term research geared to issues identified as important by HMIs or by the Government. There is now a dearth of research developing out of the concerns of the researchers themselves or addressing policies in an independent critical way. (Universities)

> The emphasis on short-term contracts for self-contained studies leads to concentration on low-level data collection yielding superficial descriptions of narrow features (rather than deeper understandings of wider educational matters). (SCRE)

The *World Yearbook of Education 1985,* reviewing educational research in 14 countries, identified increasing central control as a world-wide trend.

The solution, however, does not lie in allowing researchers to decide priorities for themselves. In the long term the best hope for research may rest with the third of Broadfoot's (1988) 'thrie estates' in education, the teachers. The important questions underlying the contribution of research to education are: what is to be researched, how is it to be done, who does it, and who decides the answers to these three questions?

The teacher as researcher

If research is to contribute effectively to educational policy and practice, the boundary between those who do research and those who use it must be lowered. The teacher-researcher movement argues for removing the boundary altogether. The basic tenets of this movement are familiar: a key principle is that teachers should review critically and systematically their own approaches to teaching and learning, gathering evidence to monitor their own practice, perhaps collaboratively in a school-based project, deciding themselves which aspects to scrutinise. Its origin is commonly attributed to Stenhouse (1975) and its development linked with the name of Elliott (1981), but the ideas are remarkably close to those practised by William Boyd in the years leading up to the foundation of SCRE (Wake, 1988). Boyd and his colleagues in the EIS saw teacher-involvement in research as a step towards full professional status: Stenhouse saw the research-oriented approach as the essential characteristic of the 'extended professional'. Schon (1983) has applied the concept to other professions in his account of the 'reflective practitioner'.

The idea need not be restricted to teachers. Educational administrators could also adopt a research-oriented approach, if they could find time (and perhaps they ought to make time for it). In pre-Region days, Directors of Education (in Fife and East Lothian especially) developed strong local research groups; and currently, at least some administrators and senior staff in schools have embarked on the arduous path of using the work in which they are professionally engaged as the basis for research studies.

Silver (1988) commented on the popularity of this approach (which, following Elliott, he termed 'action research') in his report on a review of research in education in 26 colleges and polytechnics in Britain:

> Beyond question, the most frequent emphasis, in the policies and practice of departments and in the discussions with individual staff and with groups of staff, was on the possibility of breaking through the constraints and by some form of collective or collaborative effort, and particularly through 'action research'. . . . The prevalence of action research . . . can be dismissed as either fashionable or the only option of barefoot researchers trying to keep up their morale. It is, in fact, neither. It is an extension of a growing commitment in the 1970s and 1980s to the concept of the teacher researcher, of teachers investigating their own practice, of inquiry which begins with the experience of and questions formulated by teachers themselves. . . . In becoming what Schon calls reflection-in-action, it moves inevitably into the collaborative, participatory modes. . . . Stenhouse's view of research as part of a 'community of critical discourse' becomes, in a later formulation, 'the establishment of communities of critical action-researchers'.

In her presidential address to the British Educational Research Association, Broadfoot (1988) developed a similar theme. Speaking of the 'thrie estates' in education — government, scholars and teachers (matching the traditional three, aristocracy, clergy and the people) — she said:

In recent years the yawning gulf between researchers and teachers has begun to be very effectively bridged by the advent of forms of enquiry that unite both groups in common cause. Whether through principle or pragmatism, there has been a growing tendency for educational researchers to address the issues that teachers themselves identify; to share with teachers insights as they are generated so that validation or further illumination may be generated by the latter's response. In some cases the main responsibility for the research has been handed over to teachers with professional researchers providing technical support and dissemination. As a result, many teachers have become much more interested in and supportive of the research enterprise.

The metaphor of 'three estates' is apposite in suggesting 'emancipation' as an outcome of research involvement. Improved status and power were the aspirations of the 1917 Reform Committee and the founders of SCRE, and they saw research as one of the means towards this end. But an alternative, tempting role for researchers is to enter into an alliance with administrators to form an élite technocratic group to manage the system. Though this may seem attractive, it is potentially divisive and is likely to result in a wholly subordinate role for researchers as well as teachers, their job being to carry out decisions made by others in councils from which they are excluded.

Action research, however, also has its dangers, and one danger is that it may become a bandwagon which people leap on without due considera- tion. There is a risk that this style of working may trivialise research, by restricting it within the framework of the teachers' immediate (and admittedly often limited) concerns, resulting in peripheral modifications of conventional practice and thinking. Another risk is that inexperience may result in research of poor quality, insufficiently analytical or critical or systematic — or even plainly incorrect or biassed. The movement's evangelistic style tends to encourage the idea that anyone can do research, using only a little reflection and a ready flow of language. Teachers are busy people; researchers likewise have a demanding job to do; and anyone who expects to perform both roles simultaneously must expect a heavy work load.

For research, one effect of new styles has been a loss of identity, in that the distinctiveness of 'doing research in education' is no longer as clear as in the days when experimental design and measurement were crucial. If this means a consequent loss of the rather limited respect which educational research now commands, clearly that is to be regretted. But a move away from that scientific analogy was necessary. The growth of action research has brought into prominence the question of 'What counts as research?'. Silver (1988) notes that one effect of the teacher- researcher movement has been to blur the boundary between professional development and educational research:

Is a consultancy involvement with a school . . . going to count? Are the curriculum development process and materials . . . going to count? Will the work with a group of teachers monitoring their own procedures and performance, to be written up and disseminated locally, count?

The key may be in the effect on the participants. Co-operative action which develops from a local initiative and is characterised by self-direction is more likely to result in the kind of thinking and systematic review of evidence which would justify the title of 'research'. Thus a paradoxical consequence of the introduction of staff development programmes in schools, with compulsory 50 hours annually, may be to discourage action research through over-control centrally.

Development along these lines is one way for research to strengthen its contribution to education, but not the only way. The cheese analogy suggests that we must recognise different styles of research, and different ways in which it may contribute to education. But Silver's conclusion to his report is a forecast which would have pleased the members of the 1917 Reform Committee:

> The emphasis on collaborative research and action research indicates a widespread attempt to rethink what constitutes research, how it can be launched and sustained, and what its purposes are. . . . It may not be too fanciful to describe the phenomenon as a new republic of research.

References

ADAMS, F. (ed) (1985) *Science and Computers in Primary Education.* Edinburgh: The Scottish Council for Research in Education.

BLACK, H. D. *and* DOCKRELL, W. B. (1984) *Criterion-Referenced Assessment in the Classroom.* Edinburgh: The Scottish Council for Research in Education.

BLACK, H., HALL, J. *and* YATES, J. (1987) *Assessing Modules: staff perceptions of assessment for the National Certificate.* Practitioner MiniPaper 3. Edinburgh: The Scottish Council for Research in Education.

BROADFOOT, P. (1988) Educational research: two cultures and thrie estates, *British Educational Research Journal*, 14, 3-15.

BROADFOOT, P. *and* NISBET, J. (1981) The impact of research on educational studies, *British Journal of Educational Studies*, 29, 115-122.

CRONBACH, L. J. *and* SUPPES, P. (1969) *Research for Tomorrow's Schools: a disciplined inquiry for education.* New York: Macmillan.

ELLIOTT, J. (1981) Foreword, pp 1-9. In: NIXON, J., *A Teacher's Guide to Action Research.* London: Grant McIntyre.

GETZELS, J. W. (1973) quoted in: TRAVERS, R. M. W., *Second Handbook of Research on Teaching.* New York: Rand McNally.

GIDDENS, A. (1982) *Profiles and Critiques in Social Theory.* London: Macmillan.

JOHNSTONE, M. *and* MUNN, P. ((1987 *Discipline in School: a review of* '*causes*' and '*cures*'. Practitioner MiniPaper 1. Edinburgh: The Scottish Council for Research in Education.

MCCLELLAND, William (1949) *Selection for Secondary Education.* International Examination Inquiry. University of London Press for The Scottish Council for Research in Education.

MACGREGOR, G. (1934) *Achievement Tests in the Primary School: a comparative study with American tests in Fife.* University of London Press for The Scottish Council for Research in Education.

MCPHERSON, A. *and* RAAB, C. D. (1988) *Governing Education: a sociology of policy since 1945.* Edinburgh University Press.

ROTHSCHILD REPORT (1971) *Framework for Government Research and Development.* Cmnd 484. London: HMSO.

SCHON, D. A. (1971) *Beyond the Stable State.* New York: Norton.

SCHON, D. A. (1983) *The Reflective Practitioner: how professionals think in action.* London: Temple Smith.

SCOTTISH COUNCIL FOR RESEARCH IN EDUCATION (1939) *Studies in Arithmetic: reports on investigations relating to present practice and teaching methods in the primary school,* 1. University of London Press for The Scottish Council for Research in Education.

SCOTTISH COUNCIL FOR RESEARCH IN EDUCATION (1941) *Studies in Arithmetic,* 2. University of London Press for The Scottish Council for Research in Education.

SCOTTISH COUNCIL FOR RESEARCH IN EDUCATION (1948) *Studies in Reading,* 1. University of London Press for The Scottish Council for Research in Education.

SCOTTISH COUNCIL FOR RESEARCH IN EDUCATION (1949) *Addition and Subtraction Facts and Processes.* University of London Press for The Scottish Council for Research in Education.

SCOTTISH COUNCIL FOR RESEARCH IN EDUCATION (1950) *Studies in Reading,* 2. University of London Press for The Scottish Council for Research in Education.

SCOTTISH COUNCIL FOR RESEARCH IN EDUCATION (1961) *Studies in Spelling.* University of London Press for The Scottish Council for Research in Education.

SCOTTISH EDUCATION DEPARTMENT (1965) *Primary Education in Scotland* (The Primary Memorandum). Edinburgh: HMSO.

SCOTTISH EDUCATION DEPARTMENT (1977a) *Assessment for All: report of the committee to review assessment in the third and fourth years of secondary education in Scotland* (The Dunning Report). Edinburgh: HMSO.

SCOTTISH EDUCATION DEPARTMENT (1977b) *The Structure of the Curriculum in the Third and Fourth Years of the Scottish Secondary School* (The Munn Report). Edinburgh: HMSO.

SCOTTISH EDUCATION DEPARTMENT (1983) *16-18s in Scotland: an action plan.* Edinburgh: SED.

SCOTTISH EDUCATIONAL RESEARCH ASSOCIATION (SERA) *Newsletter.* Winter 1987, 25.

SILVER, H. (1988) *Education and the Research Process — Forming a New Republic?* London: CNAA.

STENHOUSE, L. (1975) *An Introduction to Curriculum Research and Development.* London: Heinemann.

TAYLOR, W. (1973) *Research Perspectives in Education.* London: Routledge & Kegan Paul.

WAKE, R. (1988) Research as the hallmark of the professional: Scottish teachers and research in the early 1920s. *Scottish Educational Review,* 20, 42-51.

WEISS, C. H. (1977) *Using Social Research in Public Policy Making.* Lexington: Heath, Lexington Books.

World Yearbook of Education 1985 NISBET, J. (ed). London: Kogan Page.

WRIGHT, G. G. N. (1952) *The Writing of Arabic Numerals.* University of London Press for The Scottish Council for Research in Education.

3

Persistence and Change in Teacher Education

Gordon Kirk

Whether or not teachers are the pioneers of educational advance they are expected to implement in schools and classrooms whatever new strategies are agreed for the educational system. Wherever educational developments originate, they reach fruition only through the efforts of teachers. It is perhaps inevitable, therefore, that the significant changes that have taken place in education in Scotland, even since 1945, should be reflected in significant changes in the arrangements made for the professional preparation of teachers. This chapter seeks to chart some of those changes. It will explore four interrelated themes: the emergence of an all-graduate profession; the growing involvement of teachers themselves in preparation for and induction to the profession; the strengthening of SED control; and the persistent ambiguities of the institutional context in which teacher education takes place. Finally, an attempt will be made to assess the role and impact of research on the changing context of teacher education.

The emergence of an all-graduate profession

The regulations of 1905 and 1906, to which the roots of our present arrangements for teacher education can be traced, formally recognised the distinction between graduate and non-graduate teacher. According to Stocks (1986) the effect of the regulations was to reduce the role of the universities to that of 'adjuncts to the system of teacher training, rather than essential parts of it'. Those, like the EIS, who valued the university connection, continued to campaign for graduate status for all teachers and their voice was to be heard with increasing insistence in each of the major reviews of teacher education conducted since 1945.

The first of these, the report of the Advisory Council on Education in Scotland (SED, 1946), rejected graduation for all on the grounds that degree programmes, with their heavy academic orientation, were hardly 'the right way to overcome our Scottish propensity to over-emphasise school attainments and the intellectual side of education'. It was also claimed that graduation for all would mean that the training of teachers would be 'controlled by a private body, many of whose members are not in close touch with the schools'. Despite the fact that, on the basis of the evidence submitted to it, the Council claimed to represent a professional consensus, two of its members, both former presidents of EIS, signed a note of reservation which reaffirmed the case for 'a graduate profession' as the key to enhanced status and high quality recruitment.

Many of the arguments considered by the Advisory Council resurfaced in the evidence submitted to the Robbins Committee (1963). That evidence was dominated by the need to create degree opportunities for the 40 per cent or so of college diploma students who had university entrance requirements. Some witnesses advocated the creation of liberal arts colleges with degree-granting powers. However, there was majority support for 'a teacher's degree' or 'a professional degree' offered by a university. When asked if the degree might be conferred by an institution other than a university, an EIS witness replied emphatically, 'That is the one thing we want to avoid.' It was hardly surprising, therefore, that the report itself should recommend the introduction of BEd degrees, controlled by the universities, to be taken by students in colleges of education and taught for the most part by 'recognised' staff in the colleges. Before long the four largest colleges had established a relationship with their neighbouring university and the first students were enrolled.

The first cohort of students in the new BEd had not yet graduated when a third major review of teacher education was undertaken, this time by the Scottish Sub-committee of the House of Commons Select Committee on Education and Science (1970). Because of the dissolution of Parliament in 1970, that review did not result in a report. However, the published evidence it received provides a further instalment in the evolution of an all-graduate teaching profession in Scotland.

The evidence presented to that enquiry, particularly that provided by college of education representatives, demonstrated considerable discontent. It is clear that some of the colleges were finding the relationship with a neighbouring university too constraining. For example, Wood of Jordanhill College declared his commitment to 'courses designed for the job we have to do . . . and not designed in a pattern which was conceived perhaps 200 years ago'. Notre Dame College of Education and Dunfermline College of Physical Education complained of the reluctance of universities to enable them to offer BEd degrees and still others regretted the educational 'apartheid' that had been introduced by the Robbins BEd, which had separated degree students from others and differentiated between 'recognised' teachers and their colleagues.

The discontent revealed by the evidence rumbled on throughout the '70s. In 1973, Dunfermline College went to the Council for National Academic Awards (CNAA) to have its BEd in Physical Education validated. Jordanhill College followed suit in 1975. Throughout that decade, colleges increasingly took their in-service awards to CNAA for validation.

Finally, in February 1983, the Secretary of State intimated that a new four-year BEd would be introduced for primary teachers in Scottish colleges of education. That decision was influenced by several factors. Firstly, SED was aware that all-graduate entry could be secured without reliance on the universities and therefore without relinquishing any control of teacher education: colleges could secure validation through CNAA and it is known that SED officers were impressed by CNAA validation procedures. Secondly, the government was committed to a quality of teaching initiative and saw all-graduate entry as one aspect of that policy. Thirdly, the resource problem that had bedevilled discussions about the four-year degree over the years was solved by securing agreement to the strategy of increasing substantially the proportion of students entering primary teaching by the postgraduate route. Finally, and perhaps most significantly, graduate entry had been introduced south of the border. With the resolution of the issue in the primary field, it was not long before BEd degrees were available in the two remaining non-graduate points of entry — in technical education and in music — and by 1986 the ideal of an all-graduate profession in Scotland had been realised.

Growing involvement of the teaching profession in training

Teachers had, since the middle of the nineteenth century, aspired to control entry as a way of enhancing professional standing. In its early days, according to Belford (1946), the EIS sought to establish itself as that kind of professional body. When, in the 1860s, responsibility for the approval of professional credentials passed temporarily to the universities, opposition was expressed to the composition of the university examining board on the grounds, recorded by Rusk (1928), that 'the organised body of school masters should have some representation in it'. In more recent times much of the opposition to the university control of teacher education has derived from the fear that such an arrangement would weaken the involvement of teachers themselves in the training system, and give too much influence to those who were 'too remote from the actual teaching job, the job in the schools, to be really effective' (Select Committee, 1970).

The recognition of teacher involvement in the training of entrants to the profession was secured by the establishment in 1965 of the General Teaching Council for Scotland. That body, which from 1969 contained an overall majority of teachers, assumed responsibility for determining who should be finally admitted to the register of teachers and who, therefore, were entitled to teach. It was only in that limited sense that teachers 'controlled' entry, since the act which established the Council followed the Wheatley recommendation that the requirements for entry ultimately had to be determined by the Secretary of State as the guardian of the public interest.

At the same time, the Council was granted responsibility for scrutinising courses of initial training: it was expected to visit colleges of education to review programmes and could refer to the Secretary of State a college which did not respond positively to the assessment of its work. For many teachers, that power was unimpressive: for example, in his evidence to the Select Committee, Docherty of the SSTA felt that they were 'innocuous powers', having little or no impact on the autonomy of the colleges and thus failing to grant teachers a significant say in the nature of training.

That analysis of the GTC in its early years is understandable. As Inglis (1972) has shown, the Council was struggling to establish itself, and was preoccupied with standards of entry to the profession, with registration, and with the elimination of 'uncertificated' teachers. Naturally, visits to the colleges were rare. Over the years, however, visits have become more regular and through them the GTC's influence on training has increased. Influenced by evaluation studies of the apparent ineffectiveness of training conducted on its own account as well as by researchers such as Nisbet and colleagues (1977), the Council undertook, along with SED, an analysis of how the role of teachers in training could be enhanced. The resultant Sneddon Report (1978) articulated the principle of partnership in training and laid down guidelines for that partnership to which colleges have since been expected to conform. Indeed, when the Secretary of State began to issue guidelines for teacher education courses in the early '80s he was able to insist that colleges should evolve patterns of partnership based directly on the 1978 report.

It is probably true to say that since that report the GTC's influence on initial training has increased decisively, principally because colleges have come to accept that since substantial parts of teacher education pro- grammes take place in schools it is imperative that detailed agreements are reached with schools on all aspects of school experience. In addition, a significant line of research activity has reinforced the importance of the 'craft' knowledge of the teacher, the kind of knowledge that arises directly out of the teacher's ongoing work and which is a necessary complement to the theoretical knowledge gleaned from textbooks and college classes. As a result, colleges have now evolved elaborate strategies for consultation with the profession: teachers are now involved in the selection of students, in course planning and delivery, in student assessment and in course evaluation. What is more, the expectations of validating bodies such as CNAA have been such as to emphasise the part played by teachers in professional preparation. Thus, SED guidelines, the expectations of validating bodies, research evidence, as well as the intuitive conviction of teachers themselves, have all pointed to the same conclusion: teacher education requires the substantial involvement of teachers themselves in the process. Arguably, the GTC's influence has been exerted less through its own assertiveness or intrusiveness than by the willing acceptance by colleges of education of the partnership principle and of their accountability to the profession.

However, it is now clear that the powers of the GTC will be restricted to the scrutiny of academic and professional standards at the point of entry to teaching. Having rejected a suggestion made by the present writer (Kirk, 1985), the GTC missed an important opportunity to extend its powers and the Secretary of State, perhaps suspicious of a professional body that had become too politicised, has created a new body — the Scottish Committee for Staff Development in Education (SCOSDE) — with wide-ranging responsibilities in the area of teachers' professional development.

The strengthening of SED control

Responsibility for the certification of teachers passed to central government in 1872 and in the years since then SED control has always been in evidence. Kerr (1902), a former chief inspector, has recorded how, at the turn of the century, he received departmental approval to put an end to the practice of requiring students to learn by heart 300 lines of poetry. Cruickshank (1970) records the involvement of HM Inspectorate in setting the examinations for students as well as in the assessment of teaching. Indeed, until the creation of the GTC, SED carried full responsibility for the certification of teachers. That development, along with the creation of independent colleges of education with boards of studies able to play an important role in the academic decision-making process, led to some weakening of SED control. However, since the late '70s, that control has been vigorously reasserted. The Secretary of State has the authority to close a college, to discontinue a course, and to approve courses. The last of these has tended to be exercised by establishing guidelines with which proposed courses must be compatible to obtain SED approval. The justification for such guidelines is that the Secretary of State has a responsibility to ensure that colleges are providing teachers with the kind of professional preparation that is appropriate for the circumstances obtaining in Scottish schools. When the guidelines were first introduced they were developed as a consultative exercise involving colleges, regions, HMI, teachers' associations, and others. The guidelines could be said to represent a professional consensus on the main features of courses. Since the guidelines were expressed in reasonably broad terms, they provided planning teams with plenty of scope for imaginative and enterprising course design while, at the same time, ensuring a basic family resemblance between programmes associated with a particular qualification.

However, in recent years SED control has been even more prescriptive and intrusive. In areas where no guidelines exist — in physical education and in technology — SED has made stipulations about Honours degree/ Ordinary degree differentials which conflict with the professional understandings of staff. Guidelines for in-service courses are now being devised by the Secretary of State's own body, SCOSDE, apparently in a non-consultative way, with the result that colleges have to devise programmes in accordance with guidelines they played no part in shaping. Further evidence of SED's more directive role is provided by the recently mounted major initiative in school management. That initiative is being tightly controlled by SED: a team of HMI have identified the major themes as well as the staff involved in the development of the course materials. These materials will not be subjected to scrutiny by academic boards and there will be no external validation. The management of the initiative effectively reduces the colleges to the role of implementers of government policy. It is not difficult to see in such a climate how the introduction of college inspections and their public reporting is interpretable as a mere mechanism of control rather than a stimulus to development.

Finally, the various controls on the academic and professional work of the colleges are paralleled by an enormous range of constraints which restrict the freedom of colleges on financial and staffing matters. Of course, parliamentary accountability requires the careful scrutiny of the financial affairs of the colleges. However, some of the constraints exercised, for example those relating to the reporting of the hour-by-hour deployment of staff, are excessively bureaucratic and run completely counter to the idea of autonomous institutions under their own boards of governors.

The institutional context
Throughout its long history, teacher education in Scotland has been undertaken in different institutional contexts, including the churches, the universities, and the state. However, over the years, the debate on the most appropriate institutional context for teacher education has persisted.

The compilers of the 1946 Advisory Council report were convinced that preparation for the education service was 'a function of such scope and social importance that it deserves an institution to itself, an institution with a singleness of purpose which no department of a larger institution could ever have'. Conscious that they were reflecting a trend of educational opinion in Scotland, they rejected a solution which would have made teacher training a part of the work of the universities and went on to propose institutes of education. These would be major establishments 'in the van of educational advance'; they would co-operate with SCRE in promoting educational research in all its branches with the co-operation of local teachers; they would provide professional education for all concerned with the educational service — teachers, HMI, directors of education, and lecturers in further education — as well as for a range of those working in the 'people professions' — probation officers, welfare officers, and those engaging in the youth service; they would be 'the focal point of educational activities in the province', offering professional support for teachers; they would be staffed at senior level by those comparable in status to university professors, with salaries to match; and, finally, they might even take over the work undertaken by the university departments of education.

That vision of the colleges as major centres of professional education and research can be repeatedly glimpsed in the evidence submitted to the Robbins Committee and to the Select Committee. While the post-Robbins BEd was intended to foster institutional development, that degree was divisive; it tended to under-value the central professional activities of colleges; and it induced an attitude of dependence on the universities. Undoubtedly, the more potent influence on the colleges was the Robbins-inspired CNAA, which gave colleges access to professionally credible and rigorous external validation, raised their self-esteem and, by obliging them to introduce structures and procedures that provided a proper context for degree-level work, transformed their whole mode of operation. Consequently, the Scottish Tertiary Education Advisory Council (STEAC) report (1985), in commending their work, defended their continued independence, fearing their peripheralisation if they were absorbed by larger institutions.

Since the 1946 report, then, the colleges have moved some way towards the kind of institute then envisaged and, indeed, in some areas they may have moved beyond expectations then held. They have secured an acknowledged place in the spectrum of higher educational institutions; the overwhelming thrust of their work is at degree and postgraduate level; they have diversified beyond teacher education into community education, social work, speech therapy, leisure and recreation; they have become major centres for research, development and consultancy; and they offer continuing professional development opportunities and support for thousands of professionals annually. Indeed, the way is now open for them to progress towards accredited status with CNAA.

That scenario of a separate and vigorously developing college of education system is certainly attractive from many points of view, not least that of social pluralism, which advocates variety and diversity of educational provision as a way of maximising choice and of decentralising power. However, over the years the college system has suffered enormous contraction. Between 1971 and 1986 the number of students has diminished from 14,683 to 4,333; since 1977 the number of academic staff has more than halved; and since 1981 the number of of colleges has reduced from ten to five. Humes (1986) has dismissed them as weak and vulnerable institutions. What, then, does the future hold for them?

There are three alternatives to the scenario of a separate college system endorsed by STEAC: in line with the recommendations of the Beattie Report (SED, 1986a) there could be a 'radical unification of the sector', in which individual colleges become 'separate operating arms of a single educational organisation'; they could become federated or integrated parts of universities, possibly through faculties of education, a development which would be welcomed by certain sections of the teaching profession and would recognise the important role in education which the universities still perform through their MEd programmes as well as through the work of Stirling University's Department of Education; or they could integrate with the central institutions, thus building on the collaboration in course provision and the sharing of premises that currently take place, and on the recent creation of the Conference of Scottish Centrally-funded Colleges.

The irony is that, only three years after a major review of future strategy, these differing scenarios are not entirely unrealistic or implausible. Indeed, there is a sense in which recent developments are intended to perpetuate ambiguity and inconsistency. The most obvious of these is that, on the one hand, institutions are being urged to engage in the kind of collaborative activity which the three alternative scenarios imply while, on the other, they are being encouraged to be keenly competitive and entrepreneurial in their activities (SED, 1986b). Commenting on the new climate, Cuthbert (1988) likens a modern college to 'a free-ranging creature, establishing its own niche in a hostile environment through its speed of thought and action and its sharp teeth . . .'. That notion of predatory ruthlessness is not easily reconciled with that of professional collaboration. It would appear that there is a further scenario, one in which institutions are pressurised by being required to live with inconsistencies and contradictions.

The role of research
What role has research played in the developments described above? To pose that question is perhaps to reveal an expectation that an educational system should foster disciplined enquiry into its own mode of operation and that progress should depend on extensions of understanding achieved by scholarly investigation. Of course, a rationally ordered educational system of that kind, in which action is informed if not determined by research findings, is a virtual impossibility. In education, as in other complex fields of social life, action is determined by a variety of factors and influences — the impact of pressure groups, political expediency, and perhaps even the power of charismatic personalities. Research competes with these other forces as a primary determinant of policy. It should not be surprising, therefore, to find that research has played no great part in the developments described, if that term is used to denote investigative work by scholars and groups of scholars. Research has certainly played a significant role in connection with the increased involvement of the profession in teacher education: repeated evaluations of programmes have drawn attention to the theory-practice dichotomy and have pointed to the need to establish a closer integration of college-based and placement-based activities. In addition, a developing line of research has focused on the ways in which that partnership can be fostered to provide teachers with a more prominent role in placement supervision in assessment and in the furthering of teachers' professional development. In the other three areas discussed, research has been less in evidence. The critical scrutiny of practice has tended to take the form of national reviews which involved the taking of evidence and the distillation from a welter of, at times, conflicting views into recommendations for action. Arguably, it would be a useful research exercise to seek to establish the dynamics of these national commissions of enquiry and to seek to examine how particular recommendations were arrived at, as well as to assess their impact on policy in comparison with political and other forces.

References
BELFORD, A. J. (1946) *Centenary Handbook of the Educational Institute of Scotland*. Edinburgh: The Educational Institute of Scotland.
CRUICKSHANK, Marjorie (1970) *The History of the Training of Teachers in Scotland*. Edinburgh: The Scottish Council for Research in Education.
CUTHBERT, Robert (1988) Strategy and Structure. In: CUTHBERT, R. (ed), *Going Corporate*. Coombe Lodge Further Education Staff College.

HUMES, Walter (1986) *The Leadership Class in Scottish Education.* Edinburgh: John Donald.

INGLIS, W. B. (1972) *Towards a Self-governing Teaching Profession.* Edinburgh: Moray House Publications.

KERR, J. (1902) *Memories Grave and Gay.* Edinburgh: William Blackwood and Sons.

KIRK, G. (1985) The GTC and the professional development of teachers, *GTC Newsletter,* 16, February 1985.

NISBET, J. D. (*et al*) (1977) A survey of teachers' opinions on the primary diploma course in Scotland, *Scottish Educational Studies,* 9, 2.

ROBBINS COMMITTEE (1963) *Higher Education — report of the committee appointed by the Prime Minister under the chairmanship of Lord Robbins.* Cmnd 2154 (Robbins Report). Written and oral evidence, Vol C and Vol F. London: HMSO.

RUSK, R. R. (1928) *The Training of Teachers in Scotland.* Edinburgh: The Educational Institute of Scotland.

SCOTTISH EDUCATION DEPARTMENT (1946) *Training of Teachers: a report of the Advisory Council on Education in Scotland.* Edinburgh: HMSO.

SCOTTISH EDUCATION DEPARTMENT (1985) *Future Strategy for Higher Education in Scotland: report of the Scottish Tertiary Education Advisory Council.* Edinburgh: HMSO.

SCOTTISH EDUCATION DEPARTMENT (1986a) *Colleges of Education: report on financial management survey.* (Beattie Report). Edinburgh: SED.

SCOTTISH EDUCATION DEPARTMENT (1986b) *Consultation Paper on the Composition of Governing Bodies of Scottish Central Institutions.*

SELECT COMMITTEE ON EDUCATION AND SCIENCE (SCOTTISH SUBCOMMITTEE) Session 1969-70 (1970) *Teacher Training,* Minutes of Evidence. London: HMSO.

SCOTTISH EDUCATION DEPARTMENT and GENERAL TEACHING COUNCIL FOR SCOTLAND (1978) *Learning to Teach* (Sneddon Report). Edinburgh: HMSO.

STOCKS, J. (1986) Broken links in Scottish teacher training, *Scottish Educational Review,* 28, 2.

4

Research and Change in the Education of Girls and Women in Scotland

Margaret Sutherland

Democracies with a Protestant tradition are more likely than other states to provide well for the education of girls. So wrote Nicholas Hans (1949) in his classic work on comparative education. Scotland, however critical some contemporary writers may be of its claims to religious or democratic distinction, would, on this hypothesis, be a country in which the education of girls must have flourished. Is Scotland indeed in the vanguard here? What can research tell us about the present, and possible future, situation of education for girls and women? And what does such consideration tell us about research in Scotland?

International comparisons
We have to set our criteria of comparison. Throughout the world, access to education at primary, secondary and tertiary levels has improved spectacularly for females since the 1950s (UNESCO Yearbooks, *passim*). There has been a marked transition from situations in which females generally received less education than males at one or all of these levels, to the present when, in developed countries, equality of access has been achieved at primary and secondary levels and equality has been nearly achieved at the first stage of tertiary level in most of these countries. Some systems in fact have a 50:50 ratio entering tertiary education, a few even show a slightly higher percentage of female than male entrants to universities, though at the next stage (mastership and doctoral studies) women generally revert to minority status (Sutherland, 1987). Developing countries may still show female minorities at primary and secondary level.

In developed countries, with equality of access, research now focuses on a continuing sex bias in choice of subjects: it concentrates also on the links between subject choice and employment: and it turns to the career prospects of women in the world of work, their more limited range of occupations, their lower average pay and poorer chances of promotion. But other important studies are concerned with attitudes and self-concepts; and with classroom interaction which is likely to affect these. Here it has been suggested that within the equal-access co-educational classroom, boys are more likely than girls to receive attention from the teacher and are more assertive about their rights to use scientific apparatus and computers, while girls hesitate to speak out or to take initiatives. Such differences, it is suggested, affect future careers and behaviours, making mockery of the principle of equality.

At the same time recent research has indicated a rather unexpected trend (OECD, 1986): girls are more likely than boys to complete full secondary education; they tend to get rather higher marks than boys in end-of-school examinations, or to be more successful in achieving school certificate qualifications.

In Scotland, has the situation of girls and women in education, careers and social status undergone similar transformation? Or was the Scottish situation already so democratic that no change was needed? What light does research throw on these questions of equality of access to various levels of education and employment, and on attitudes to them?

Girls in the Scottish educational system
Our data do show changes and indicate a need for change.

Access to primary and secondary education has not been a problem. Annual reports on Education in Scotland, (SED, *passim*) show fairly even number of boys and girls entering junior and senior secondary schools. Further, Nisbet and Entwistle (1966) indicated in their study of the appropriate age for transition to secondary schools that sex differences in maturing did not seem likely to introduce unsatisfactory bias, though results depended on the kind of test used. Yet we can see a minor but interesting influence on girls' secondary education in the system of 'exemptions' by which in years following the Second World War young people could be excused attendance after the age of 14 if otherwise serious hardship would be caused in their homes. Looking at the figures from 1947 to the early 60s we see diminishing use of this provision but girls usually outnumbering boys in the ratio of 4 to 1 (SED, 1947-1963). (Studies of truancy usually still show domestic circumstances affecting girls' absenteeism.) In general, in the 1950s girls seem to have tended to leave secondary school earlier: and this can be associated with social attitudes prevalent at the time.

We can also find evidence of some enthralling differentiation within secondary education. Emphasis on courses in homecraft for girls was to be expected in the 1950s and is clear in the annual SED Reports: but there were also differences in mathematics courses in the junior secondary school, frequently with separate classes which were not, as in modern experiments, to try to improve girls' achievements but to enable boys to learn arithmetic, algebra and geometry while girls concentrated on arithmetic, 'with some mensuration and graphs'. Not altogether surprisingly, given the attitude apparently prevailing, it was noted that in senior secondary examinations a majority of maths candidates were boys (SED, 1958).

Access to university education has, alas, followed the trend common to most other European countries in the first half of this century: women students have been in a minority. After the initial positive action following the 1892 decision that Scottish universities should admit women students, and after progress to a women students' percentage of 23.7 by 1910 (Cunningham, 1980) the years between the wars, and for some time after, showed a kind of plateau. Women students' percentage of approximately 27 in 1938 and 1947 had by 1961 risen only to 31 (Robbins Report, 1963). (Surprisingly perhaps, women at that time outnumbered men in further education and, by no means surprisingly, they outnumbered men in teacher training which absorbed 4 per cent of the qualified group of women, 0.3 per cent of men.) The Robbins Report did comment that in Scotland the proportion going on to higher education (males and females) was 9.3 per cent compared with 8.2 per cent in England and the proportion of women entering university was higher than in England.

Such a difference has continued in recent years, the proportion of women in Scottish universities being just a little higher than in English: in 1987, the percentage of women among full-time students in Scottish universities was 40.6 and in English universities, 39.9 (UGC, 1986-7). Among first entrants to universities in 1976-77 women were 41.1 per cent in Scotland and 35.7 per cent in England, rising in 1986-87 to 44.5 per cent in Scotland and 41.4 per cent in England. (The corresponding rise for Wales was from 38.6 per cent to 46.6 per cent!) Such minor differences cannot obscure the fact that, despite improvement, both Scotland and England compare poorly with other 'developed' countries, for example France, Finland, Canada, the United States, Poland, where the 50:50 ratio has been reached: and this difference cannot be ascribed to policies which make, or do not make, the professional education of teachers part of university education. At postgraduate level in Scottish universities similarly the percentage of women is scarcely inspiring — 30 per cent full-time and 31 per cent part-time in 1986-7 — while among Scottish university teaching staff, 2.4 per cent of women at professorial level is lower than the English universities' 2.8 per cent and decidedly lower than the percentages in other European countries (unsatisfactory as these also are (Sutherland, 1985)).

Two reservations should perhaps be made here. One is that obviously not all women students in Scottish universities are Scottish nor all women students in English universities, English. It is unlikely that this materially affects the picture given. The second is that numbers of Scottish women students have opted for Ordinary rather than Honours degrees. The Ordinary degree, though it has its own merits, is likely to provide less competitive qualifications in the graduate labour market.

Yet Scotland has been a leader in the trend for girls to achieve better qualifications than boys in secondary education. It is difficult to know precisely at what point this change-over occurred, especially as much depends on whether one 'counts' Highers or Lowers or 'O' grades or Certificates of Sixth Year Studies or any number or combination of these. For 1961, the Robbins Report noted (just before the introduction of 'O' grade) that:

> the difference in performance between boys and girls is far less in Scotland than in England and Wales. About nine girls obtain 2 Highers and 3 Lowers for every ten boys who do so, and the proportion of girls who obtain university entrance qualifications is about 80 per cent of the proportion for boys, as compared with about 60 per cent in England. If the qualifications of school leavers are compared with the number of children staying at school till 17, it appears that the performance of those who stay on to a given age is, in Scotland, considerably better for girls than for boys.

(This indicates that girls were then less likely to stay on than boys. Increased retention rates of girls in full-time secondary schooling, and more girls than boys now staying on, may suggest a growing inequality, to the disadvantage of boys, even when employment prospects are taken into account.)

For whatever reason, this good performance by girls in secondary schools continued. In 1964 (SED), in the 3 Higher and 2 'O' grade category, girls outnumbered boys; considering Highers only, girls were more numerous than boys; but boys were more numerous at the four Highers level. Although slightly larger percentages of girls than boys continued to gain 1-2 or up to 4 Highers, it was only in the 1980s that girls having 5 or more Highers equalled (and in 1986 slightly surpassed — 11 per cent to 10 per cent) boys. The difference at the other end of the scale is clearer: in 1986, 78 per cent of girls leaving school had gained some certificate qualification compared with 72 per cent of boys: and this disparity had already been present for some years.

One must regret that research has not shown whether earlier differences were due to school policies, teachers' attitudes or pupils' self-confidence; and whether present trends are determined by employment prospects or mainly by social or environmental pressures. A recent analysis by Willms and Kerr (1987) of examination results since 1976, while confirming the development of superiority in girls' performance, did also indicate a rural-urban variable and the importance of social class differences.

Research and gender differences

But beyond the data of official reports, what else has research during SCRE's sixty years revealed about girls and their education?

SCRE investigations themselves, as a reading of Craigie (1972) confirms, have often focused on problems requiring practical, though research-backed, solutions — problems of selection for different types of secondary education, the use of tests, the appropriate age of transfer — as well as on general surveys of attainment in different types of school, or potential for attainment. Gender differences have not been regarded as a main issue. (Indeed, Powell's (1985) admirable investigation deliberately opted to study teachers as individuals rather than categorise them by gender — in some ways, a good principle.) Thus the earlier SCRE reports evince a kind of dispassionate, rather uninterested recognition of gender differences. Happily, most of these reports, unlike others of the time (and some in the present time), do at least state whether there were differences in the performances of males and females, even if they did not regard these as necessarily calling for a change or adaptation in educational policy (see, for example, Earle's (1937) recognition of different variances in girls' and boys' performance in standardised tests of English and maths; or the analysis (SCRE, 1986) of English and maths performance in primary schools, 1953-1963).

Girls and the National Surveys

Those classic national studies, the Scottish Mental Survey of 1932 and the follow-up of 1947 (SCRE, 1949), did indeed find interesting gender differences. (In passing, have we forgotten what a good unit Scotland is for such surveys? And would such research today be able to count on so much voluntary and skilled co-operation from so many people?) Yet the investigators did not take much to heart the observed differences in performances on tests of intelligence. What appeared was that there might be a slight difference between girls' and boys' intelligence as measured by the Stanford-Binet test in 1932, the girls' being lower. (A slightly later survey of about 1000 children (MacMeeken, 1939), tested by one tester only, found that the average IQ of both boys and girls was 100 — or, to be precise, 100.5 for boys , 99.7 for girls.) The 1947 Survey gave more complicated results. Results from the sub-sample tested by the Terman-Merrill revision of the Binet test gave a boys' mean of 104.4, a girls' mean of 100.7, a significant difference. But on the group test (whole population) the girls' score was higher than that of the boys, 37.62 as opposed to 35.88. Both boys' and girls' scores were in fact rather better on this test in 1947 than in 1932, but whereas the boys' score had gained 1.37 points, the girls' had increased by 3.21 (Maxwell, 1961).

But the main concern of the research had been to discover whether differential fertility was producing a *decrease* in the national intelligence: consequently, the evidence of a possible sex difference was not regarded as of major concern (nor was the dscrepancy between intelligence test results and the 27 per cent of women among university students in 1947). Test theory of the time was indeed ready to accept a possible sex difference in mainly verbal tests and in tests with performance items or items involving spatial or other abilities. But we have to note that this apparent superiority of 11-year-old girls in verbal group tests of intelligence (later known as verbal reasoning tests) has been widely found and has had considerable practical consequences, in England and Northern Ireland, for authorities determining 11+ selection procedures. The decision has often been to establish separate norms, or separate lists, for boys and girls, so that the boys would not be disadvantaged by what was assumed to be a temporary superiority of the girls. Similar considerations have led to separate lists where teachers' estimates, especially of 'suitability', have been used. But where such procedures continue, there are now queries as to whether this means injustice to girls — they have to achieve higher scores than boys to have equal chances of access. One recent commentator (McQuaid, 1988) indeed has suggested that the performance of girls in secondary schools indicates that their superiority at 11+ is genuine, not a passing phase, so separate lists should be abolished and, in fact, a court ruling has now imposed the same qualifying mark for both sexes in Northern Ireland (TES, 1988).

It seems a pity that research at the time did not explore such issues and consider, for instance, why girls' scores showed gains from 1932 to 1947 — hypotheses as to earlier age of puberty, or test sophistication, do not seem to cope with all the differences noted. But gender differences were not then a popular theme — in research as in other consumer goods there is the 'flavour of the year' (or decade) phenomenon.

Following-on
Yet the admirable follow-up of a Six-Day Sample over the next sixteen years did offer useful insights into the prospects and attitudes of both gender groups as they progressed through school and into employment. What differences were noted?

James Maxwell (1969), analysing follow-up data, reported that for those girls leaving school at the earliest opportunity, 'the number of avenues of training are fewer and better defined than for the boys'.

Further education taken by girls was mainly in commercial subjects; other noteworthy training was for nursing and hairdressing. 'A lower proportion of girls leaving in 1951 continued their education than boys leaving in the same year, 11 per cent of girls against 31 per cent of boys.'

For those leaving in 1954 or 1955, the girls' 'pattern varies from the boys' mainly in terms of opportunities offered.' Although access to university was open to both groups, non-graduate teacher training and nursing were mainly for girls. Thus while 32 boys went to university, only 6 girls obtained a university degree.

In later employment, the female group differed from the male both in the absence of National Service requirements at that time, and in the effect of marrying:

> For the men it has been noted that marriage has not a very marked effect other than having a certain stabilising effect on their employment progress. This is not so for the women. Marriage is a clearly marked milestone in their careers, and in most cases it means the giving up of their employment after a longer or shorter interval.

Teachers had been asked to assess sample members on various desirable personality traits. Though no detailed analysis was made, it was found that girls generally received a more favourable rating than boys. Weston's (1984b) later finding that girls reported spending more time on homework than did boys and had generally rather more favourable attitudes to school seems to suggest a continuing difference in the two groups' responses and behaviours.

Leisure interests also seem to have been similar to those found in later studies (Countryside Commission for Scotland, 1985): considerably more men than women engaged in playing some sport: 45 per cent of men and 71 per cent of women engaged in none. There was some indication that women, more than men, joined uniformed organisations such as Guides, and were slightly more involved with Church groups. Maxwell makes a good point in citing the 22 year-old woman with five children who said 'that she had little leisure: she spent what free time she had visiting her parents.'

Longitudinal studies of this kind are to be cherished, though one recognises the difficulties, not only of finance and security of employment, that they present to a research team: it is a pity this one stopped there. But we have some information as to whether the impression of girls and women following much the same patterns as those in other European countries continued to be true, since, fortunately, systematic surveys carried out by the Centre for Educational Sociology in the University of Edinburgh provide data on these patterns in subsequent decades.

Recent trends

Burnhill and McPherson (1984), reporting on returns from 1971 and 1981 surveys of academically well-qualified school leavers, found a marked change of attitude towards careers for women not only among the female respondents but also among the males — 'Qualified women have become more ambitious, educationally and occupationally, and more men and women are now prepared to accept such ambitions as legitimate.' Notably, a marked change seemed to have occurred in women's expectations about their working life. Whereas the earlier group expected periods of full-time or part-time work, intermittently, with only 15 per cent expecting work full-time 'for most of my working life', the 1981 population showed 40 per cent expecting to have this career pattern. Similarly there had been a shift in the attitudes of both men and women with regard to women's careers, showing a reduction in the belief that women could derive as much satisfaction from their husband's career as from their own, and an increase in the belief that a career could offer a woman as much satisfaction as having a family. At the same time, in 1981, 34 per cent of men and 30 per cent of women agreed that 'men are not keen to marry "career" women.'

But attitudes to careers must be associated with work prospects for all, not only for the well-qualified. Recent surveys (Raffe, 1984, 1988) of the fate of school leavers in general show that there are still considerable differences in the kind of occupation typically entered by young women and young men. This, or the lingering effect of tradition, may link to the very considerable sex bias still evident in the choice of school subjects (Weston, 1984a), with girls still opting more for languages and boys more for science. Certainly the employment prospects for girls seem to differ from those of boys, with staying on at school to gain qualifications apparently improving girls' chances of finding a job. But so many changes have been made in recent years with schemes for the employment of those leaving school at 16 — YOP, YTS, two-year YTS — that it is difficult to be sure whether observed trends will continue or be changed by new schemes or new conditions in the labour market. It does seem clear, however, both that females still tend to be concentrated in a smaller number of occupations than males, and that finding and entering employment does differ for males and females in Scotland.

Another continuing difference is the greater proportion of able young women who opt to become teachers, and this despite the evidence (Corr, 1980; Cruickshank, 1970; SED, 1975 and SED, 1986) that women teachers' salaries and chances of promotion have long been less good than those of men, even allowing for differences in career duration, and despite what could be folk memories of the marriage bar (Adams, 1987).

The Scottish situation has been unique since the 1924 regulations which made a university degree obligatory for men wishing to obtain a General Teacher's Certificate. Women alone were left with the possibility of taking the less prestigious and, in the past at least, the academically less exacting qualification given by college of education studies only. For various reasons — perhaps the relative shortness of time required or belief in college courses' greater 'relevance' to their future work — women took the college route with considerable enthusiasm. The recent reduction in the number of places available may finally have brought some such women to apply for university entrance, thus in part increasing the proportion of women undergraduates. Recent preferences for a later age of marriage and beginning a family, noted by Burnhill and McPherson, may also be influential. Some changing trends in subject choices are evident, and recent developments may scarcely have improved the appeal of teaching. But we have to note that the apparently less academically demanding option fitted with the self-deprecating attitude of women which various researches (McPherson *et al,* 1972; Sutherland, 1981) have found: more women than men, apparently, have doubted their ability to cope with university studies. Is this also changing?

Conclusions
Altogether, available research findings have not been in line with expectations of a more democratic, egalitarian situation for women in Scottish education. Admittedly, we lack the kind of information provided by many recent studies in England and the States about classroom interactions. Are Scottish girls generally as vocal as boys in such situations? How far do teachers' attitudes and school organisation still reinforce differentiation of role and expectations of future studies and employment (even if textbooks are scrutinised for sex bias, and exam questions are carefully non-sexist)? Possibly some answers to these questions are available in MEd and similar dissertations (certainly MEd students in various option courses are made aware of research on this matter in other school systems); but MEd research evidence at present — sometimes very unfortunately — tends to be lost to the wider circles of scholarship. It would be interesting to know whether some Scottish schoolgirls are as down-trodden, crushed, sexually harassed as apparently some English schoolgirls are. Yet in seeking such evidence we would want to avoid the defects of some of the small-scale 'illuminative' research now widely publicised in this area. All too frequently isolated instances, the experiences of one or two individuals or a small group of schools, are cited with no indication that these findings cannot reliably be generalised. Thus the dramatically 'sexist' or 'racist' remark achieves widespread currency, however unrepresentative it may have been. Number-

crunching has its faults as research, illuminative case studies and oral history have their merits: but the possible weaknesses of these also have to be kept in mind and recognised.

Our survey of the educational situation of girls in Scotland thus leaves us mainly with the impression that it does not differ much from the situation in other European or 'developed' countries. We find improved access to education, improving standards of attainment, concentration in the teaching profession, and a generally rather restricted range of occupational choices, but some changing attitudes to career and marriage. Indeed without any great surge of feminist publicity, much the same kind of evolution seems to have gone on in Scotland as elsewhere: though we rather lack evidence as to underlying attitudes.

What kind of research has been useful and is likely to be useful in future? There is obviously a lot to be said for the systematic, large-scale monitoring of educational performance from year to year — or at reasonable intervals (the Thatcherite proposals for systematic testing may have *some* merits). Document analysis research on official statistics and reports is similarly important. Like systematic surveys it is not glamorous, and it may seem uninspired, but it is useful and, on the whole, it makes fewer demands on funding (a point sometimes overlooked by teams of civil servants or government-appointed committees who feel they must go abroad to seek at first-hand what is already well documented). Above all, systematic monitoring shows whether educational policies and practices are changing, are having the intended effects or possibly producing some unforeseen and rather undesirable effects. Further, the simple publication of such surveys may affect the attitudes of those deciding and implementing present policies. (Have UNESCO publications recorded or stimulated the improvements in women's access to education? The present collection of data on the situation of women employees in Australian universities is certainly regarded as part of Affirmative Action to reduce inequalities.)

Equally, we need qualitative studies (carefully designed) to discover what underlies some of the unexpected, or even the expected, events shown by monitoring. Our review has shown how various gender differences have been neglected in the past. We need research to show the effects of new techniques, new teaching methods, the study of a new subject or integrated subjects: do they affect both gender groups — or other groups — identically? Research is equally needed to show the attitudes and value judgements of teachers, learners, parents, administrators of education. And since, as we have seen, the education of women shows common features in many countries, international links and comparisons must sharpen researchers' perceptions.

Such research may not immediately produce massive changes in national policies or society's attitudes. But we do need to know what the situation, as distinct from social or political rhetoric, is: which variables are determining it; whether, in the case of women's education and employment, there is continuing progress or regression. Research thus remains worthwhile — and fascinating.

References

ADAMS, C. (1987) *Teaching — a Celibate Profession: a study of the marriage bar on women teachers in Scotland 1915-1945*. Unpublished MEd dissertation. University of Glasgow.

BURNHILL, P. and MCPHERSON, A. (1984) Careers and gender: the expectations of able Scottish school-leavers in 1971 and 1981. In: ACKER, S. and WARREN PIPER, D. (eds) *Is Higher Education Fair to Women?* pp. 83-115. Guildford: SRHE and NFER-Nelson.

CORR, H. (1983) The sexual division of labour in the Scottish teaching profession, 1872-1914. In: HUMES, W. M. *and* PATERSON, H. M. (eds) *Scottish Culture and Scottish Education*, pp. 137-150. Edinburgh: John Donald.

COUNTRYSIDE COMMISSION FOR SCOTLAND (1985) *Scottish Leisure Survey, Report 1*. Perth.

CRAIGIE, J. (1972) *The Scottish Council for Research in Education 1928-1972*. Edinburgh: The Scottish Council for Research in Education.

CRUICKSHANK, M. (1970) *A History of the Training of Teachers in Scotland*. London: University of London Press for The Scottish Council for Research in Education.

CUNNINGHAM, S. (1984) Women's access to higher education in Scotland. In: ACKER, S., MEGARRY, J., NISBET, S. *and* HOYLE, E. (eds) *World Yearbook of Education 1984: Women and Education*, pp. 173-187. New York: Kogan Page.

EARLE, F. M. (1936) *Tests of Ability for Secondary School Courses*. London: University of London Press for The Scottish Council for Research in Education.

HANS, N. (1949) *Comparative Education*. London: Routledge and Kegan Paul.

MACMEEKEN, A. M. (1939) *The Intelligence of a Representative Group of Scottish Children*. London: University of London Press for The Scottish Council for Research in Education.

MCPHERSON, A., FLETT, U., *and* JONES, C. (1972) *Women Entrants to University and College of Education — Some Competing Explanations*. After Highers Project, Research Paper 1. University of Edinburgh, Sociology Department.

MCQUAID, C. (1988) Doubts cast on 11+ as a measure of ability. *The Times Educational Supplement*, 18 March 1988.

MAXWELL, J. (1961) *The Level and Trend of National Intelligence*. London: University of London Press for The Scottish Council for Research in Education.

NISBET, J. *and* ENTWISTLE, N. J. (1966) *The Age of Transfer to Secondary Education*. London: University of London Press for the Scottish Council for Research in Education.

OECD (1986) *Girls and Women in Education*. Paris: OECD.

POWELL, J. L. (1985) *The Teacher's Craft*. Edinburgh: The Scottish Council for Research in Education.

RAFFE, D. (ed) (1984) *Fourteen to Eighteen*. Aberdeen University Press.

RAFFE, D. (1988) The status of vocational education and training: 2: the case of YTS. Paper presented to the ESCR/DE workshop on *Research on Employment and Unemployment,* London, 29 January 1988. University of Edinburgh, Centre for Educational Sociology.

ROBBINS COMMITTEE (1963) *Higher Education: report of the committee appointed by the Prime Minister under the chairmanship of Lord Robbins.* (Robbins Report). Appendix 1, 24. London: HMSO.

SCOTTISH COUNCIL FOR RESEARCH IN EDUCATION (1949) *The Trend of Scottish Intelligence*. London: University of London Press for The Scottish Council for Research in Education.

SCOTTISH COUNCIL FOR RESEARCH IN EDUCATION (1968) *Rising Standards in Scottish Primary Schools: 1953-63.* London: University of London Press for The Scottish Council for Research in Education.

SCOTTISH EDUCATION DEPARTMENT (1975) *Differences of Provision for Boys and Girls in Scottish Secondary Schools*. A report by HM Inspectors of Schools, Edinburgh: HMSO.

SCOTTISH EDUCATION DEPARTMENT See annual reports on *Education in Scotland* for the years cited. Edinburgh: HMSO.

SCOTTISH EDUCATION DEPARTMENT See *Statistical Bulletins* for the years cited. Edinburgh: Government Statistical Service.

SUTHERLAND, M. B. (1981) *Sex Bias in Education,* p. 90. Oxford: Blackwell.

SUTHERLAND, M. B. (1985) *Women Who Teach in Universities*. Stafford: Trentham Books-European Institute of Education and Social Policy.

SUTHERLAND, M. B. (1987) Sex differences in education: an overview, *Comparative Education,* 23, 1, pp. 5-9. In this issue, see also articles by MOORE, K. M. *and* ELIOU, M.

TES (TIMES EDUCATIONAL SUPPLEMENT) (1988) More transfers, (p. 8, 12 August). *Ibid* (23 September 1988) Court gives girls places at grammars.

UNESCO *Statistical Yearbooks*. Paris: UNESCO. See also UNESCO: *Higher Education: international trends 1960-1970.*

UNIVERSITY GRANTS COMMITTEE (1987) *Statistical Record 1986-87,* 1, *Students and staff*. Cheltenham: University Statistics.

WESTON, P. (1984a) Learning their place: differentiation and the S3/S4 curriculum in practice and prospect. In: RAFFE, D. (ed) *Fourteen to Eighteen,* pp. 25-27. Aberdeen: Aberdeen University Press.

WESTON, P. (1984b) Reviewing compulsion: pupil perspectives on the fourth year experience. In: RAFFE, D. (ed) *Fourteen to Eighteen*, pp. 58-78. Aberdeen: Aberdeen University Press.

WILLMS, J. D. *and* KERR, P. D. (1987) *Changes in Sex Differences in Scottish Examination Results since 1976*. University of Edinburgh, Centre for Educational Sociology.

5

Has Schooling a Future?

David Hamilton

These are uncertain times. The present government has tabled proposals that, if implemented, represent a fundamental restructuring of schooling. Considerable controversy, not to say opposition, has been aroused by these proposals. Indeed, it is an open question whether we are living in times of transition or times of crisis. Certainly, the future of schooling remains unclear. For instance, is the restructuring process a temporary and transient phenomenon? Or is it, instead, the harbinger of an extended period of innovation and upheaval? Likewise, what are the political currents that underpin such proposals? Should the restructuring process be regarded as a centralising initiative — a power play to keep schooling on its 'true' course? Or should it, instead, be regarded as a decentralising initiative — a redistribution of power that will enable schools to negotiate their own educational futures?

These thoughts about the current status of schooling derive from the convergence of two research interests. First, a recurrent concern to make sense of contemporary changes within schooling (see, for instance, Hamilton, 1977; Hamilton, 1988). And secondly, a broader concern to appreciate the ways in which, through the ages, schooling has been linked to other social institutions such as the family, the church, the state and the labour market (see, for instance, Hamilton 1987a; Hamilton, forthcoming). From both research standpoints I have treated schooling as a historically-located social institution. I recognise, accordingly, that it is a human invention: it was originally designed — and has been repeatedly adapted — to meet the challenge of new social circumstances and new human aspirations. To explore these dynamic aspects of schooling, my research programme of the last ten years can be described as a series of mapping exercises. When and where, for instance, did schooling first take shape? And by what routes and readjustments has it arrived at its present configuration?

But, it might be asked, what has been the educational purpose of such inquiries, given that they appear to dwell disproportionately upon the practices of the past? The answer to this question is the same as that given for any kind of time-series analysis. Insofar as history can be thought of as the study of change rather than the investigations of the past, all historical research necessarily illuminates the distinctiveness of the continuous present. Reflecting upon my own work in such terms, I have been repeatedly drawn to the question: 'if schooling has a beginning and a middle does it also have an end?'.

In the beginning
From the privileged standpoint of the twentieth century, 'schooling' can be readily differentiated from 'education' insofar as its associated practices of teaching and learning are highly formalised and standardised. Schooling owes its existence, that is, to a normative framework that reaches beyond the organisation and administration of individual schools. Hence, it is not the historical appearance of 'schools' that marks the emergence of schooling but, rather, the appearance of networks of schools guided by an external discipline of rules and regulations.

In the European context, the notion of a common discipline of schooling came to prominence in the twelfth century. It arose from a struggle between the Church and a range of secular rulers who also claimed stewardship of God's earth. To re-affirm and extend its political influence, the Church undertook to overhaul its administrative apparatus. Specifically, it sought to replace self-perpetuating clerical dynasties with a more committed cadre of career administrators. The unwanted persistence of clerical dynasties was addressed in a variety of ways. Post-ordination celibacy was made compulsory by the second Lateran Council (1113); child recruitment (oblation) was banned among the newly-founded religious orders (e.g. the Cistercians and Cluniacs); and the purchase of direct entry to monastic houses (simony) was outlawed by the Fourth Lateran Council 1215).

In return, the Church exploited a new source for its administrators — the talented progeny of lay families. And to train these near-adult recruits, the Church set about expanding and modifying its existing complement of cathedral schools. Previously, cathedral schools were associated with groups of scholars who devoted themselves to the examination and elaboration of theological texts. Indeed, the major philosophical movement of the Middle Ages — scholasticism — took its name from such schools. The reformed cathedral schools, however, had a more immediate purpose. They were never intended to produce philosophers. Rather, they were to turn out a body of foot soldiers capable of patrolling the Church's front lines. And the soldiers' task — as parish priests — was the enforcement rather than the interpretation of canon law.

To support these developments, the Church made a major investment in education and training. For instance, the Third Lateran Council (1179) and its immediate successor agreed, respectively, that church-approved schoolmasters need not pay for their licences, and that cathedrals and other large churches should make special financial provision for the support of in-house teachers of grammar and theology (cf Latin and canon law). At one level — namely the spread and stabilisation of cathedral schools — these changes can be regarded simply as the culmination of centuries of official exhortation. But at another level (viz schooling's new social mission), they represented a clear break with the past. In effect, the philosophers and their disciples took themselves off to the newly-founded universities (e.g. Paris), leaving the cathedral schools to a less-elevated (and newly-named) type of teacher — the *magister scholae*, and leaving these teachers to a new and less-mature population of 'pupils' (an alternative translation of the Latin word *Discipuli*).

From European Church to nation states

Despite the hegemonic efforts of the medieval Church, various nation states eventually rose to political and economic prominence. In France, for instance, the fifteenth century is marked by a continuous struggle between the national interests of the French King and the wider interests of the Catholic church. Among other things, the dispute hinged upon the University of Paris' claim — derived from Papal decree — that its property and personnel were beyond the King's jurisdiction. In the event, the University was forced to surrender its privileges. Thereafter, universities, colleges and schools — throughout Europe — gradually began to conform to national rather than international priorities. The fifteenth-century invention of moveable-type printing also played a part in this nationalising tendency. The reduction in unit printing costs not only allowed texts to be produced in vernacular languages (e.g. the Latin/English *Grammar* compiled by the first High Master of St Pauls, William Lily), it also facilitated the penetration of such texts into previously unvisited territory.

By the middle of the sixteenth century Church and state had begun to capitalise upon these new opportunities. Official edicts, for instance, repeatedly enjoined England's 'schoolmasters and teachers of grammar' to use 'none other' than Lily's *Grammar* (see Charlton, 1965, page 108). And, more generally, schooling began to be identified as a powerful means of intervening in the upbringing practices of any and all social groups. Faced by the social, economic and political challenges of the Reformation (e.g. unemployment, inflation, heresy) schooling was, itself, to be reformed. Above all, it was to take on an evangelising remit (see, for instance, Strauss, 1978). National populations were to be converted, en masse, to a new set of social, economic and moral principles. In Calvinist Scotland, *The Book of Discipline* (1560) recorded these aspirations. The 'reformation of religion', so its preface claimed, was necessary for the establishment of 'common order and uniformitie' throughout the realm (quoted in Cameron, 1972, pages 87-88). And, to this end, *The Book of Discipline* indicated that all parents were to be 'compelled to bring up their children in learning and vertue' (page 132).

Such a policy was not only politically apposite, it was also pedagogically feasible. By that time, its implementation could be based upon readily-available texts, upon a recently-formalised teaching method (viz. catechesis); and, not least, upon the adoption of a curriculum derived from a freshly-formalised map of knowledge (see, variously, Hébrard, 1983; Dhotel, 1967; and Hamilton, 1987a).

From spiritual salvation to social progress

Typically, sixteenth century reformers proclaimed the correctness of such policies on the grounds that they conformed to scriptural truths — 'God's written and revealed word' (Cameron, 1972, page 86). As the years passed, however, politicians emphasised a new source of authority. God's intentions, they claimed, were to be found not only in the books of the Bible but also in the workings of nature. Moreover, they argued, the workings of nature were decipherable with the aid of another God-given device — reason. Thus, as the century of Luther, Calvin and Knox turned into the century of Bacon, Descartes and Newton, statecraft was driven by two new but related considerations. First, that due attention should be given to identifying the laws of nature. And secondly, that comparable attention should be given to the restructuring of social institutions in conformity with such newly-found norms.

For the leaders of Church and state, then, the advancement of science and the development of schooling were opposite sides of the same coin. Both offered leverage upon the social and spiritual elevation of humankind. In effect, seventeenth-century political theorists were the first to recognise that, without delivery, there could be no deliverance (see, for instance, Oestreich, 1982). The writings of Jan Amos Comenius (1592-1670), a Protestant minister born in Bohemia and educated at universities in the Netherlands and Germany, clearly illustrates this outlook. In *The Great Didactic* (1632) Comenius elaborated his fundamental belief that, properly ordered and organised, schooling could teach 'all things' to 'all men'. Moreover, Comenius' presumption of methodological infallibility was no idle claim. If the pedagogic organisa- tion of time, subject matter and method could be harnessed to the 'order' of nature then, so Comenius claimed, schools would be 'as free from friction' and 'as free from failure' as any other 'automatic machine'.

Claims about the managerial value of 'order' also figured in Comenius' discussion of larger organisational units. *The Great Didactic*, for instance, not only identified the 'universal' requirements of teaching and learning, it also sketched out an administrative framework for the management of state-wide school systems. Further, in *Panorthsia* (1644), Comenius proposed that there should be custodians of law and order in 'every school', 'every church' and 'every state'. Specifically, the supervision of schools was to be the responsibility of a 'tribunal of the learned' who, among other things, would attend to the methods, books and teaching used in such schools (see Hamilton, 1987a).

Bolstered by this joint appeal to scriptural authority and natural reason, schooling was gradually reconceptualised as a unitary and unified instrument of social policy. The networking of schools, that is, gave way to beliefs about the systematisation of schooling. And, over the same period — the publication of John Bunyan's *Pilgrim's Progress* (1678) is a useful marker — the notion of schooling as a source of spiritual salvation gradually gave way to an eighteenth-century Enlightenment concern for schooling as an agency of social progress. During the next 200 years, the organisation of schooling did indeed take on many of the features outlined by Comenius. And it is probably no accident, therefore, that the first English-language edition of *The Great Didactic* appeared in 1896 — a time when schooling in Britain (and elsewhere) was undergoing extensive remodelling in the interests of systematisation (for the Scottish evidence see Finn, 1983).

Schooling and beyond

Over the same period, schooling had a conceptual and organisational coherence. First, it became accepted as an organ of the political state. Secondly, the transformation of children into citizens became accepted as the political purpose of schooling. Thirdly, it was accepted that the state could deploy a web of regulatory instruments to keep schooling responsive to its political interests. And finally, it became accepted that system-maintenance should be the responsibility of a cadre of state officials apart from the main body of teachers.

For at least 450 years, therefore, the organisation of schooling was underpinned by a vision of social regulation *cum* social transformation. Of course, conceptions of the state have changed (see, for instance, Gordon *and* White, 1979), the web of regulatory instruments has changed (see, for instance, Foucault, 1979), and definitions and categories of citizenship have changed (see, for instance, Hadow, 1923). Equally, seventeenth-century notions about the political importance of spiritual redemption are not the same as twentieth-century notions about the political relevance of social welfare. Nonetheless, I submit that there is an important continuity between the vision of schooling held by Calvin and Comenius and that held by Boyd, Rusk and the other pioneering spirits of the SCRE.

But 1928 is not 1988. Is the thinking behind the reform proposals of the late 1980s the same as Boyd's and Rusk's? Are educational institutions to be made more socially efficient by realigning the overall system? Or is the same goal to be achieved by dismantling the system? Currently, different elements of the reform package appear to pull in different directions. As noted earlier, proposals regarding the 'opting out' of schools seem to signify a political concern to weaken the state control of schooling. Yet, on the other hand, proposals regarding the establishment of a national curriculum seem to foreshadow increased state regulation.

What is the status of this apparent contradiction? Should the reform package be understood as an uneasy merger of individual politician's wish lists? Or should it be appreciated as a sophisticated model of political devolution — a rationale whereby social institutions can both opt out and remain within the purview of the political state? The available evidence — largely press leaks and the coded language of ministerial statement and parliamentary debate — seems to support the former explanation. Politicians who favour opting out do not appear to share a common framework with those who call for a strengthening of the national system of curriculum and assessment. The opters-out (or 'neo-liberals') seek to shift the locus of political control away from the epicentres of local and central government. In turn, they wish schools to be regulated under the pressure of local and national market forces. And, overall, neo-liberals base their view of the future upon a strengthening of the school-economy nexus.

By contrast, politicians who favour nationalisation of the curriculum (viz the 'neo-conservatives') seek to relocate power in the Downing Street Cabinet Room. In their turn, they advocate a prescriptive model of bureaucratic and fiscal regulation. And, above all, they place great store upon strengthening the links between schooling and citizenship. As already noted, neo-conservative arguments are well grounded in history. They resonate, for instance, with *The Book of Discipline* (1560), with Fichte's *Address to the German Nation* (1807-8) and with the concern for post-sputnik national security that informed the curriculum legislation of the American National Defense Education Act (1958). In practice, however, neo-conservative thinking has signally failed to establish agreement over what might count as a national curriculum. By default, then, its associated conception of citizenship has become eclipsed by the neo-liberal conception of 'enterprise'. Yet even here a fundamental difficulty arises. There is probably as little public agreement over what counts as an enterprise culture as there is over what counts as a national curriculum.

So where, then, does this leave schooling? From an historical perspective, the following broad observation seems relevant. Failure to agree upon either the substance of a national curriculum or the attributes of an enterprise culture can be seen, ultimately, as a further weakening of the concept of Scottish nationhood. To speak of a national curriculum is to presume, for instance, the authority of a national church (or its equivalent). A multicultural or pluralist curriculum would, quite literally, be inconceivable to Calvin or Comenius. Likewise, both theorists would have great difficulty in grasping the notion of an enterprise curriculum. For Calvin and Comenius, universal schooling was intended to inculcate the values of public service and personal piety, not those of private enterprise and market-led consumption. Indeed, the notion of free will — the ultimate source of twentieth-century conceptions of human enterprise — was explicitly denied by both Calvin and Luther (see Wendel, 1965, pages 272 & 190; and Hamilton, 1987b).

In these terms, then, the 'beginning' and 'middle' years of schooling were sustained by an ethical framework that no longer seems to command the same measure of political acceptance. It is hardly surprising, therefore, that the recently-tabled policy package has come into conflict with popular presumptions about Scottish schooling. Given the events of the past, it is probably no exaggeration to say that these proposals are as pivotal to late twentieth-century schooling, as the first *Book of Discipline* was to the political context of the mid-sixteenth century. Should we, therefore, have cause to remember them as a *New Book of Discipline?*

References

CAMERON, J. K. (ed) (1972) *The First Book of Discipline.* Edinburgh: The Saint Andrew Press.

CHARLTON, K. (1965) *Education in Renaissance England.* London: Routledge and Kegan Paul.

COMENIUS (1644) Panorthsia. In: HAMILTON (1987a). The pedagogical juggernaut, *British Journal of Educational Studies,* 35, 18-29.

COMENIUS, J. (1896) *The Great Didactic* (1632). London: Adam and Charles Black.

DHOTEL, J. C. (1967) *Les Origines du Catéchism Moderne d'après les Premiers Manuels Imprimés en France.* Paris: Desclée de Brouwer.

FINN, M. (1983) Social efficiency progressivism and secondary education in Scotland 1885-1905. In: HUMES, W. M. *and* PATERSON, H. M., (eds) *Scottish Culture and Scottish Education 1800-1980.* Edinburgh: John Donald.

FOUCAULT, M. (1979) *Discipline and Punish: the birth of the prison.* Harmondsworth: Penguin.

GORDON, P. *and* WHITE, P. (1979) *Philosophers as Educational Reformers: the influence of idealism on British educational thought and practice.* London: Routledge and Kegan Paul.

HADOW, W. H. (1923) *Citizenship.* Oxford: Clarendon Press.

HAMILTON, D. (1977) *In Search of Structure: a case study of a new Scottish open plan primary school.* London: Hodder and Stoughton.

HAMILTON, D. (1987a) The pedagogical juggernaut, *British Journal of Educational Studies,* 35, 18-29.

HAMILTON D. (1987b) *Schooling and enterprise: some historical observations.* Paper prepared for the Center for Educational Research and Innovation of the Organisation for European Economic Co-operation and Development, Paris.

HAMILTON, D. (1988) *Enterprise: a conceptual and historical analysis.* Paper presented at the Annual Conference of the British Educational Research Association, University of East Anglia.

HAMILTON, D. (forthcoming) *Towards a Theory of Schooling.* London: Falmer Press.

HEBRARD, J. (1983) L'Evolution de l'espace graphique d'un manuel scolaire: le "Despautère" de 1512 à 1759. *Langue Française,* 59, 68-87.

OESTREICH, G. (1982) *Neostoicism and the Early Modern State,* Cambridge: Cambridge University Press.

STRAUSS, G. (1978) *Luther's House of Learning: the indoctrination of the young in the German Reformation.* Baltimore: Johns Hopkins University Press.

WENDEL, F. (1965) *Calvin: the origins and development of his religious thought,* London: Collins.

6

Vocationalism and Economic Recovery: the Case Against Witchcraft

Ian Stronach

Watch out Japan. Here comes Tracy Logan. Tracy Logan is a typical British sixteen year old, leaving school this year. But to Japan, and our other international competitors, she's a big threat . . . That's because this year she'll be starting two years paid skill training on the new YTS . . . Tracy will be spending the next two years learning how to take trade away from them for a change.
(MSC advertisement for the new 2-year YTS, *Guardian*, 28.1.86)

. . . the initiand begins as a person on whom no-one depends, and through the course of initiation becomes one on whom the welfare of the entire cosmos hinges. Every time a woman is initiated, the world is saved from chaos, for the fundamental power of creativity is renewed in her being.
(*Emerging from the chrysalis. Studies in rituals of women's initiation,*
B. Lincoln, 1981)

On the one hand Tracy Logan: on the other the Navajo Indian. In each case, cosmos out of chaos, and a personal transformation that carries within it the promise of a general recovery. The purpose of this chapter will be to reduce the distance between these two figures in transition, and to challenge the opposites of modern/archaic and rational/ritual that appear to divide them. For which is the more fictional character? In the context of vocationalist ideologies in the UK in the 1970s and 1980s, we cannot be sure.

If we are to bring these two figures together, then we must first set other things apart. Above all we must question the means/ends, cause/effect assumptions that relate the modern education and training of the individual to broad economic goals. It will be argued that behind these 'rational' connections lies a sleight of hand. To take the vivid example of Tracy, she is invested with a magical agency concerning an economic problem. The means/ends rationale is clearly unbelievable in itself — and so we cannot read the message in literal terms. Instead, a symbolic reading is required, in that the parts that stand for the whole (Tracy, skills, certificate, training) are taken to cause the whole (economic recovery, overtaking foreign competition). 'Standing for' becomes confused with 'causing', and so synecdoche masquerades as explanation.

Why does that elision contain even a possibility of conviction for the reader? After all, attempts to blame a military defeat on indiscipline in the Brownies would be discounted. This explanation of vocationalism will rest on the nature of ritual rather than ideology, and on the way that certain rituals of induction 'stand for' reaffirmed adult values, and address an adult 'congregation' (Rappaport, 1968, page 1) rather more than the youthful participants:

> The individuals are, to this extent, objects used in the ritual, rather than its central focus through which the ritual is to be explained. Initiation rituals cannot be understood simply as a means of changing the status of individuals.
> (La Fontaine, 1985, page 104).

Of course, that sketch of an interpretation relates to a 'mere' advertisement, but the 1986 White Paper on Education and Training shows the same kind of rhetorical features.

The White Paper

The White Paper (Department of Employment and Department of Education and Science, 1986) offers a remarkably succinct view of vocational education nested within a psychological theory, which in turn is contained within an economic argument.

The economic argument is this. Britain has serious economic problems because of a lack of competitiveness. The reasons do not involve investment or resources — 'The same machines and equipment are available to all.' (1.3) Therefore the problem is one of people. People lack motivation and training. Thus the economic problem boils down to national deficiencies in personal attitudes and skills: 'We live in a world of determined, educated, trained and strongly motivated competitors. The competition they offer has taken more and more of our markets.' (1.1) The economic remedy is to promote higher 'standards of performance, of reliability and quality. It is these which will make the critical difference to the design of British products and services, their delivery, after-sales service, customer relations and marketing and, not least, management.' (5.37)

The heart of the solution is psychological: 'Motivation is all important so that attitudes change and people acquire the desire to learn, the habit of learning, and the skills that learning brings.' (1.4)

Given that psychological climate, the vocational outcomes become possible. These are 'the three essential elements of preparation for competence in any field of employment: skills; knowledge and understanding; and practical application.' (2.11) The outcomes depend on effective learning which is relevant to employer needs. Such learning is relevant, active and practical, like TVEI: 'the provision of technical and vocational education in a way which will widen and enrich the curriculum, and prepare young people for adult and working life.' (3.1)

It is worth examining the main features of this nested vocational-motivational-economic rhetoric and its location in education-economy debates.

Juvenalise and personalise the problem

The White Paper's case rests on an economic assumption that recovery mainly depends on improved motivation and skills amongst the young. Thus change means 'regeneration' in a double sense that is axiomatic across the debate — '. . . most children could do better . . . the country urgently requires them to do better because as a nation we survive on our brains and our skills.' (Maureen O'Connor in the *Guardian*, 7.10.86); 'Mr Lawson said that one of the most long-standing problems in Britain was the failure to prepare school leavers adequately for work' (*Guardian*, 20.3.85). Within academic commentary, Prais argues that there is an intermediate 'skill gap', that education is failing the less able in comparison to achievement levels in Maths in Germany and Japan (Prais 1981, 1985), while Cantor argues for more basic skills in core subjects (Cantor, 1985). The 1985 joint conference of NIESRC/PSI/RIIA concluded 'that the economic performance of Britain may be impaired by faults of tradition and practice in its education system; and that, despite a number of policy initiatives in the last few years . . . there is need to do more' (Carter, 1985, page 7).

In addition, both the problem and the solution are personalised by the White Paper in terms of the individual attributes that young people lack. Indeed, personification extends to rival countries as well — 'determined', 'educated', 'trained', 'strongly motivated' (1.1). Presented in these terms, the person is invested with a tremendous agency in terms of the nation. She is responsible, and all the mediations of natural resources, investment policies, class, gender, race, organisational structures, and historical legacy, fall away. In vocationalism, the individual stands naked before History. There is a similar tendency towards personification in more academic debates on the connections between the economy and education — except it is the qualities of the 'worker' that are criticised (Nichols, 1986; Senker, 1986).

Assert the certainty of the problem and its solution

The White Paper maintains that a successful economy is based on high productivity, which is the result of the good quality and right mix of education and training for the young. Prais refers to the 'many decades' of the problem, while Peston comments: '. . . we have always known what to do; therefore, there must be very deep reasons why the problems persist' (Peston, 1985, page 76). And indeed Wellens prescription (Wellens, 1963) retains a contemporary feel: a 'bridging' occupational training of a general kind between school and work, the abolition of apprenticeship and its replacement with a competence-based system, emphasis on learning rather than teaching situations, an end to gender discrimination, greater mobility across the training tracks, and the need for industry to value and invest in training for workers and management. As the _Economist_ wearily noted of the 1984 MSC/NEDO report:

> The recommendations are boringly familiar; firms should invest more in their human capital; governments should have a strategy for training (and provide money to match); education should prepare young people for working life. Even the contradictions are predictable — reports usually combine a paean to the German system of vocational training (where the state plays a major role) with support for the American one (where it doesn't). (_Economist_, 8.9.84).

Further conundrums are also ignored. For example, Germany and Japan are deemed successes. The former has a major scheme for state supported training; the latter has not. So either we should do more state training, or less. And Japan is moving away from vocational content in education — '. . . effectively Japanese training begins with employment' (Peston, 1985, page 83). Indeed, the UK is moving towards the German pattern, just when the pace of change may demand 'in-house' training by industry, along Japanese lines.

Privilege the reality of work
The idea of education as preparation for work has become rooted in contemporary development. Work experience, whether 'real' or 'simulated', becomes a major strategy, as in contemporary TVEI initiatives, YTS provision, or European Community projects. Work is projected as a paramount reality — and education becomes an initiation into that 'truth' (Stronach, 1984).

Understate more parsimonious causes
Within education-economy debates there are, of course, discrepant voices. Quite apart from Marxist and neo-Marxist critique, and philo-sophical opposition, there is much contradictory empirical data in the conventional economic discourse. For example, the Handy Report (Handy, 1987) argued the case against the quality of British management (only 12.5 per cent of managers with degrees), while the 1985 MSC survey pointed to the very low investment in training by British industry (0.15 per cent of annual turnover invested in training). Nichols criticised

the scapegoating of the British worker, maintaining that UK analysts have been over-preoccupied with worker attitudes rather than management qualities (Nichols, 1986). Peston argued for a much more radical understanding of the problem — recognising the role of public schools, Oxbridge, the examination system, and the educational culture (Peston, 1985; see also Weiner, 1981). Within industry, he noted the 'chronic tendency to undervalue skill (including, above all, on-line managerial skill)' (Peston, 1985, page 78).

Senker's review of the potential relevance of TVEI changes for economic performance was pessimistic: 'Deficiencies in management education and training seem more significant than any "disease" curable by TVEI' (Senker, 1986, page 298). He also offered a telling internal comparison: '. . . the experience of Japanese firms in this country has been that the training of white-collar workers presents more problems than the training of blue collar workers' (*ibid*, page 302).

A further criticism would be that the grounds for *any* of the comparisons of single factors are unclear, as Roderick and Stephens point out:

> The links between the education system and the rest of the social structure are peculiar to the society concerned. Separate analysis of the economy and education, therefore, if used to explain differential levels of economic performance, may lead to over-simplified accounts and optimistic hopes, through quick changes in educational policy, of rapid alleviation of malfunction, the roots of which lie in complex interrelationships between a wide range of social institutions whose characteristic quality may depend on the apparent vagaries of historical development. (Roderick *and* Stephens, 1981, page 63).

Certainly, Blaug is reluctant to speculate about precise correlations between economic success and skill levels: 'No economist of education has ever successfully quantified the notion of required skill levels to achieve stated targets of economic growth'. He dismisses Prais' theory as an 'appeal to our emotions' (Blaug, 1985, page 131). Nevertheless, if it is an emotion, then it is an emotion to which many economists succumb.

To conclude: some things are clear. It is clear that the UK is preoccupied with a notion of economic decline. Evidence of that decline is decisive in relative terms: UK productivity is about half that of the US, and was surpassed by West Germany round 1960 (Worswick, 1985). But then the focus blurs. As Cantor points out, we know that Germany and Japan do more training than we do, and so there is a 'prima facie case' for increasing training and improving education.

Other things are far from clear. Indeed it is remarkable — and a measure of the quality of our democracy — how little of that complexity and contradiction can be found in the popular political debate about how education can (or cannot) contribute to economic recovery. On *a priori* grounds, it seems that the least parsimonious attributions are the most favoured. The problems defined in the White Paper concern industrial design, service, marketing, and management (5.37), yet the solutions invoke highly mediated and controversial linkages with the education of the young. Neither the logics nor the emprics of that case are compelling.

That would be a conclusion from within the discourse — that is, accepting the rationality and doing no more than trying to establish a balanced judgement. What conclusions can we come to about the discourse itself? It is to that question that we finally turn in this section.

How rational is the debate?

Weber defined rationality thus: 'methodical attainment of a definitely given and practical end by the use of an increasingly precise calculation of adequate means' (Gerth *and* Mills 1948, page 293). The definition, at heart, is progressive. But the features of the discourse are recurrent rather than progressive, and persistently divergent rather than convergent. Clearly, the discourse does not offer rational paths in terms of Weber's criteria for rationality.

Secondly, the White Paper in particular offers an intense personification of the problem, both at individual and national level. The direct mediation between individual attributes and national destinies sets up a simple logic locating responsibility in the attributes of an aggregate of individuals — a highly voluntaristic and individualistic theory of transition, in which groups are no more than the aggregate of individuals.

Thirdly, the personification of problem and solution sets up two polarities — the first is between individual identity and socially desired qualities, or 'sociocultural personhood', as anthropologists have it (Poole, 1982, page 103); the second is between the implied polarities of the adjectives — strong/weak , competitive/non-competitive, motivated/ unmotivated. These polarities carry very simple explanations of the 'problem' at their negative poles, and prescribe equally simple 'solutions' at the positive end. They are discursive structures on which much of vocationalism rests.

Fourthly, the personalising of economic competitiveness (be motivated, get skilled) offers both an economics of recovery and a metonymics of blame (if *you* were trained and motivated *we* wouldn't be where we are today). Thus the rhetoric explains youth unemployment while prescribing economic success, aligning both these phenomena on the simple polarities we have outlined. The possibility that youth unemployment may be a consequence rather than a cause becomes hard to envisage in the schema.

As a result the solution takes on a reassuring (or terrifying) simplicity:

good education/training = higher worker productivity = economic success.

The White Paper turns out to be a peculiarly selective reduction of a contradictory economic discourse. We are left with the question: what explains the plausibility of this fractured rationality? In this connection we may note the wonder expressed in the *Golden Bough* by Frazer about the old European fire-festivals that sought to prevent disease and bring good crops:

> How did it come about that benefits so great and manifold were supposed to be attained by means so simple? In what way did people imagine that they could procure so many goods or avoid so many ills by the application of fire and smoke, of embers and ashes. (Frazer, 1913, page 329).

Rationality and ritual

This chapter began with Tracy, and her personal transformation that also stood for a more general economic recovery. That kind of personification was also found in the economic-educational connections of the 1986 White Paper. The economic warrant for the policy outlined in the White Paper did not appear to make sufficient sense, and the case against youth and for vocationalism was highly selective; there was a 'remainder' left over that could be attributed to error, ideology, or — it was signalled but not argued — ritual. It is to the appropriateness of 'ritual' to an understanding of vocationalism that we now turn. Can a deficient rationality be a sufficient ritual?

'Ritual' is to anthropology as 'curriculum' is to education. Turner sees ritual as a storehouse and a powerhouse: '. . . multi-faceted mnemonics, each facet corresponding to a specific cluster of values, norms, beliefs, sentiments, social roles, and relationships within the total cultural system of the community performing the ritual' (Turner, 1981, page 2). La Fontaine offers more of a 'hidden curriculum' model, rejecting any insistence on the presence of repetitive or formalised behaviour, and stressing that we should not look for a single meaning, or even audience, for ritual: '. . . a mould into which many meanings can be poured' (La Fontaine, 1985, page 84). It is that broad definition of ritual that is most useful to this discussion.

But rituals are also like curricula in that they address needs — life stages, crisis, exorcism and cure. So there is a second question: where might we seek analogies?

Obviously, initiation rituals are relevant to transition, since youth in our society is inducted into a series of training and educational stages. La Fontaine offers a list of typical features of initiation rituals. Initiation is like a play, with some idea of the 'ideal' usually involved. It is highly symbolic, and can have many layers of meaning. Unlike a play, however, it is purposeful 'it aims to affect the world' (page 184), and includes tests, secrets, and the common themes of sexuality and birth. These, she feels, are not procreative symbols but metaphors for social reproduction; their data — fire, sex, water, yeast — all transform to other things, and are 'generative; they create change' (page 189).

Female initiations may be of particular interest for a reason that Lincoln indicates. He argues that female initiations are often concerned with the 'fundamental being' of the woman (Lincoln, 1981, page 103). That concern is three-fold: to make the girl into a woman, to renew society, and to renew the cosmos. In comparison, it could be argued that our transitions may also fail to offer new status. A concern for 'being' might be an obvious alternative (eg work experience and the emergence of its personal development rationale).

There is a final point to be made. Sometimes ritual addresses crisis. Hobsbawm points out that 'we should expect it [invented tradition] to occur when a rapid transformation of society weakens or destroys the social patterns from which "old" tradition had been designed' (Hobsbawm *and* Ranger, 1983, page 4). Elsewhere, Meyerhoff offers the example of the Wirikuta. They are agrarians who pine for their former status of hunters and their lost homeland. Their drug-centred 'peyote' rituals celebrate the First People and the deer that they once hunted: their rituals are a form of economic nostalgia (Meyerhoff, 1978). Turner also offers an extreme circumstance:

.... where norms conflict; where values are discrepant, and respectable persons find themselves compelled by circumstances to become rule-breakers; where the very axioms of society appear to be ineffective in preventing the outbreak of bitter disputes — then people experience a sharp sense of insecurity, even panic. In this social atmosphere charges of withcraft and fears of ancestral wrath are generated and proliferate' (Turner, 1981, page 89).

Thus far, it can only be argued that 'ritual' has a loose heuristic value for understanding vocationalism. The parallels are provocative rather than compelling, and a more detailed exploration is needed. The following argument tries to relate specific aspects of the structure of vocationalist debates to the complex nature of ritual as symbolic, value-laden, role-based and 'telic' — 'its design as a system of ends and means' (Turner, 1981, page 3). It is argued that features such as personal transformation and universal salvation are connected in ways characteristic of ritual accounts; that there is also a close analogy in the play of opposites and the moulding of attitudes; and that the notions of recurrence and a return to eternal values are central to ritual knowledge and vocationalism. Finally, the logical structure of the vocationalist debate will be compared with that of ritual explanations.

Individual transformation and universal salvation
As we have seen in the case of Tracy, and of the White Paper, individual and general outcomes are distinctively related in vocationalism. Personification is the typical metaphor, and it is used to make individual young people responsible for general recovery. Individual qualities are asserted as the determinants of success (e.g. Prime Minister Thatcher 14.5.88: 'thrift', 'self-reliance', 'enterprise' etc). Exemplary individuals are held up to illustrate this process, and it is no coincidence that the re-issue of Samuel Smiles' *Self-Help* had an introduction written by Sir Keith Joseph (Smiles, *ed.* Bull, 1986). The pattern of exemplary individuals is similar to the vocational strategies of the Victorian period, when 'Boyhoods of Great Men' (eg Edgar, c.1850) typified the instructive convention.

The structure is similar to that found in many rituals:

> The ritual remedy thus invoked itself possesses a form similar to the whole process of crisis and redress. It originates in trouble, proceeds through the symbolization of trouble and feelings associated with it, and concludes in an atmosphere of re-achieved amity and co-operativeness, with the hope of restored health, prosperity and fertility. (Turner, 1981, page 52).

Just as in some forms of vocational profiling, the ritual moves the individual from 'experiential selfhood' to 'social personhood' (Harris, 1978, page 63; Poole, 1982), creating an archetype of the young citizen/worker in a series of idealised personal qualities (self-reliant, enterprising, thrifty, problem-solving, reliable etc). Eliade termed this process 'the transformation of man into archetype through repetition' (Eliade, 1954, page 37). At the same time, ritual typically associates a personal with a cosmic pole, round which prosperity, morality and civilisations are clustered — and against which disorder and chaos are arraigned.

The play of opposites and the moulding of attitudes
The logic of the archetype is to create poles of negative and positive attributes. Thus, for example, profiling offers this sort of range (Stronach *et al*, 1982):

. . . the Ideal Worker, the Celestial Citizen. Or their negative shadows . . .

—self-reliant	—with guidance, can understand consequences of actions
—quick and accurate at complex calculations	—has to be given simple instructions
—adept at most kinds of verbal encounter	—speed well below industrial requirements
—can independently derive, implement and evaluate solutions	—makes little effort
—copes sensibly with moral dilemmas	—ordinarily obedient complying by habit
—sensitive to others' perceptions	—is aware of own personality and situation

The focus is personal — the 'egocentric interpretation of misfortune', as Clyde Mitchell put it in discussing the discourse of witchcraft (Mitchell, 1982, page 383). Such simple and stark dichotomies are common in ritual explanations. 'Litima' (personality, motivation) is opposed by 'bunyali' (competence and ability); 'kutama' (the worthwhile and desirable in life) by 'kuwala' (La Fontaine, 1985; Turner, 1982). For the Navajo, the 'Blessingway' opposes the 'Enemyway':

Blessingway	Enemyway
propriety	chaos
safety	monsters
civilisation	masturbation
cosmos	
sexual maturity	

(Lincoln, 1981)

The notion of moulding and shaping is also common to both ritual and vocationalist accounts. In vocationalist ritual as in 'archaic' practice, the novice has to learn to define and shape the self against an ideal— 'the presentation of the self to the self' (Harris, 1978, page 146). The process of moulding expresses transformation:

The girl is molded so she will be beautiful. Being beautiful in this case, however, implies more than having a good figure. It means that the girl will be strong, ambitious, and capable of enduring much. The molding affects the girl's personality as well as her body. It implies that she will be friendly, unselfish, and cheerful; it means she will be a kind mother and a responsible housekeeper. A 'beautiful' girl, therefore, is not only physically appealing, she is also 'good' and 'useful'. (Lincoln, 1981, quoting Frisbie, pages 94-5).

In that account, the symbolism is vivid: minor physical actions stand for great changes at different levels, from the personal to the cosmic. Again, there is a parallel with vocationalist debates, where, as we have seen, the gaps between means and envisaged ends are so large that they are difficult to understand in terms of error or even ideology. The case of the Yurok Indians reported by Erikson offers an analogy. Young Yurok Indians are encouraged to 'think rich' while eating salmon, so that hunger might be avoided, and good runs of salmon up the rivers assured: 'Such ritualizations lifted to the level of a kind of oral hallucination certain nostalgic needs which were cultivated throughout life and ceremonially intensified under ritual conditions' (Erikson, 1978, pages 80-1). The key is the condensation and intensification of a cultural imperative, in one case 'salmon'; in the other 'enterprise'. The effect is hallucination — whether economic or educational.

The symbolic Centre, recurrence, and return to eternal values.
Earlier, the 'privileging' of the reality of work was pointed out. In mini-companies, work experience, curriculum design and pedagogical strategy, the 'reality' of work determined the nature of education and training. The emergence of work as a 'paramount reality' to be experienced in order to be learned about, echoes the 'sacred Centre' of ritual — the mountain or temple wherein the sacred is the outstanding reality. But the paramount reality of work experience is symbolic — it is not more real than other curriculum events: like ritual reality, it is paramount because it is exemplary; it stands for a truth but is not itself that truth.

Recurrence — often around the 'symbolic centre' of work — is the dominant feature of vocationalist initiatives. The problem, as the economists noted, recurs. Attempts to address it recur — in the Schools Council Industry Project (SCIP) and the Education for the Industrial Society Project (EISP) in the late 1970s and early 1980s, in YOP and YTS, in TVEI and TVEI Extension and CPVE. Within initiatives, reforms recur — the TVEI initiative is really more than 100 projects, each of them working more or less independently on similar changes like IT, work experience, and profiling. Indeed, the notion of recurrence is written into the rhetoric of the initiative, belonging to the logic of 'ownership'. Nor do these attempts to define and solve the problem build on each other in any obvious way (eg in terms of a Weberian rationality).

It is not cynical to argue that these initiatives are essentially responses rather than solutions to the 'problem'. As responses, they are seen to address the problem. Ideologically, that is what is most important. But the notion of repetition does not imply failure. In ritual terms, it is necessary for success. The re-enactment is as logical as it is to put on a play more than once. It is the performance that is important, and the audience rather than the actors or the plot. In this account, our vocational initiatives are also contemporary dramas that ritually involve young people in enacting solutions to economic decline. The values they invoke are largely traditional and nostalgic: they undertake the repetition of the cosmogony — The Great Time, the Golden Age, the 'divine economy' (Eliade, 1954, page 100). Vocationalism therefore repeats its projects because they succeed at the level of ritual, however badly they fare in 'rational' terms. The 'heritage' industry, Hobsbawm's critique of 'invented tradition' in the UK, the invocations of Samuel Smiles and mythicised Victorian values are part of this ritual or regeneration wherein Britain can once more, in the words of the White Paper, become the 'envy of the world' (1.7).

The rationality of rationality
Personification in metaphor makes for circularity in logic. The first principle of the circularity is that objections to the basic theory can be met one by one, since an aggregate theory of individuals is proposed. That is to say, each individual will succeed or fail according to the degree to which she holds the appropriate qualities: the notion that individuals are one of a class (young, female, black, northern) is suppressed.

The second principle is that contradictory evidence can always be met by extending the circle of the theory. Thus lack of employability in the late 1970s rested on poor attitudes in the young, and a lack of experience of the disciplines and realities of work. Programmes of correction were set up, but the problem of unemployment grew worse. Longer programmes were introduced in order to provide the necessary skills and qualities. Six months, one year, then two years. At the same time, the criticisms of schooling grew, and prevocational initiatives entered the schools in order to remediate the problem at its source. Each expansion of the circle — Polanyi calls it epicyclical elaboration — confirms the original diagnosis, while conceding that the problem is more profound than first thought. A further elaboration of this logic would be to propose earlier school leaving, on the grounds that young people gain little from

from that stage of education, and would benefit more from vocational training or work experience. This has already been proposed (Carter, 1985).

The third principle is that the basic synecdoche at the heart of the discourse does not allow any other explanations in its own terms. Once the idea of individual qualities is set up to 'stand for' economic prosperity, there are few alternatives within the logic of the discourse (we may only argue 'which qualities?' or 'how transferable?'). Thus the welter of other possible explanations offered by economists and educationalists are either ignored or treated as separate issues.

Polanyi discusses the effects of such logics: 'Circularity, combined with a readily available reserve of epicyclical elaborations and the consequent suppression in the germ of any rival conceptual development, leads to a degree of stability to a conceptual framework which we may describe as its completeness' (Polanyi, 1958, pages 286-294). His discussion is based on an analysis of Zande witchcraft belief, but the same sorts of self-fulfilling rhetorics are evident in vocationalism. There is, therefore, nothing bizarre about the claim that the logics of witchcraft and the structures of ritual invest vocationalist debates, although their presence should not reassure us.

Conclusions

(1) The power of vocationalism is unreasonable — in terms of its own rationality. Part of its persuasiveness is ritualistic. Those rituals are embedded in the rhetoric and also enacted as multifarious 'projects' such as TVEI, CPVE, and YTS. Thus the means/ends backbone of the vocationalist discourse is 'telic' mainly in the ritual sense (Turner, 1981); that is to say, it is metaphorical and dramaturgical, enacting change and recovery, reassuring leaders and led that the world can be saved. Hence a certain potency to the symbolism, the personification, the reduction and intensification of the problem and solution. They are coherent because of the circular logics and dramatisations of ritual.

(2) This kind of 'unreason' is not based on rational error, or simply on ideological duplicity. It centres on a need to reassure the powerful as much as it seeks to mystify the powerless — and indeed the evidence seems to be that it succeeds better at the former. Marxist critiques which see in these events only mystification and manipulation of the young miss an important set of meanings; and by failing to recognise ritual for what it is, they participate in it (through oppositional accounts such as this). The difference is important. In the end the polemical contrast between the points of view of ideology and ritual about the role of the powerful is this: 'ideology' believes that they are clever and they are out to deceive us;

'ritual' believes that they are stupid and they are out to deceive themselves.

(3) But that does not mean that we confront ritual and only ritual. Rationality, ideology and ritual are all present: each has its own space and purpose. Economic rationality addresses decline, its means are better skills and attitudes in the young, and its end is economic prosperity . The socially productive rationality of the 'process' curriculum addresses motivation, its means are participative management procedures at all levels, and its end is change. Ritual addresses crisis, its means are rhetorics, projects and vocational rites, and its end is reassurance. Thus vocationalism is not one single thing, to be 'found out' amongst a range of possibilities: centralisation, mystification, recovery, ritual, hegemony, a new 'discipline' of and for youth, or even contemporary magical thinking. Nor is it equally all of these things. We should not decide too quickly that vocationalism stands for technological progress and sociotechnical advance, rather than a more archaic recovery. After all, rites of regeneration and rebirth are held to originate in Early Man's symbolising of the cycles of the moon: '. . . the complex symbolism of periodic regeneration . . . has its foundation in lunar mysticism' (Eliade, 1954, page 64). And so the tin plates of TVEI may also turn out to be the 'fingernails of the moon':

> The old men in the villages remember when first they saw some 'Malay' hunters after birds of paradise who travelled south of the village but did not come into it: they came from the west . . . they carried guns and showed the Gnau salt (the Gnau mistook it for their semen), matches and tin plates which, to the Gnau, shone like the moon and they called them 'fingernails of the moon'. (Lewis, 1980, page 200).

Note
This paper is a selective summary of a longer account entitled 'Education, vocationalism and economic recovery: the case against witchcraft'.

References
BLAUG, M. (1985) Comment. In: WORSWICK, G. D. N. (ed) *Education and Economic Performance*. Joint Studies in Public Policy 9. National Institute of Economic and Social Research/Policy Studies Institute/Royal Institute of International Affairs. Aldershot: Gower.
CANTOR, L. (1985) A coherent approach to the education and training of the 16-19 age group. In: WORSWICK, G. D. N. (ed) *op cit.*
CARTER, C. (1985) Implications for policy and research. In: WORSWICK, G. D. N. (ed) *op cit.*
DEPARTMENT OF EMPLOYMENT *and* DEPARTMENT OF EDUCATION AND SCIENCE (1986) *Working Together — Education and Training.* Cmnd 9823. London: HMSO.

EDGAR, J. G. (c. 1850) *The Boyhood of Great Men Intended as an Example to Youth.* London: Routledge and Sons.
ELIADE, M. (1954) *The Myth of the Eternal Return.* (Translator: W. Trask). New York: Pantheon.
ERIKSON, E. (1978) *Toys and Reasons: stages in the ritualisation of experience.* London: Marion Boyars.
FRAZER, J. G. (1913) *The Golden Bough: a study in magic and religion.* Pt 7 *Balder the beautiful,* vol. 1. London: MacMillan.
GERTH H. *and* WRIGHT MILLS, C. (eds) (1948) *Character and Social Structure: the psychology of social institutions.* London: Routledge & Kegan Paul.
HARRIS, G. G. (1978) *Casting out Anger: religion among the Tanta of Kenya.* Cambridge: Cambridge University Press.
HERDT, G. H. (ed) (1982) *Rituals of Manhood: male initiation in Papua New Guinea.* University of California Press.
HOBSBAWM, E. *and* RANGER, T. (1983) *The Invention of Tradition.* Cambridge: Cambridge University Press.
LA FONTAINE, J. (1985) *Initiation.* Harmondsworth: Penguin.
LEWIS, G. (1980) *Day of Shining Red: an essay on understanding ritual.* Cambridge: Cambridge University Press.
LINCOLN, B. (1981) *Emerging from the Chrysalis: studies in rituals of women's initiation.* Cambridge: Harvard University Press.
MARWICK, M. (1982) *Witchcraft and Sorcery.* (2nd ed) Harmondsworth: Penguin.
MEYERHOFF, B. G. (1978) Return to Wirikuta: ritual reversal and symbolic continuity on the peyote hunt of the Huichol Indians. In: BABCOCK, B. A. (ed) (1978) *The Reversible World: symbolic inversion in art and society.* Ithaca: Cornell.
MITCHELL, J. C. (1982) The meaning in misfortune for urban Africans. In: MARWICK, M. *op cit.*
NICHOLS, J. (1986) *The British Worker Question: a new look at workers and productivity in manufacturing.* London: Routledge & Kegan Paul.
PESTON, M. (1985) Comments. In: WORSWICK (ed) *op cit.*
POLANYI, M. (1958) *Personal Knowledge.* Chicago: Chicago University Press.
POOLE, F. J. P. (1982) The ritual forging of identity: aspects of person and self in Bimin-Kukusminmale initiation. In: HERDT, G. H. *op cit.*
PRAIS, S. J. (1981) Vocational qualifications of the labour force in Britain and Germany, *National Institute Economic Review,* 98, 47-59.
PRAIS, S. J. (1985) What can we learn from the German system of education and vocational training? In: WORSWICK, G. D. N. (ed) *op cit.*
RAPPAPORT, R. A. (1968) *Pigs for the Ancestors: ritual in the ecology of a New Guinea people.* New Haven: Yale University Press.
RODERICK, G. *and* STEPHENS, M. (1981) *Where Did We Go Wrong? Industrial performance, education and the economy in Victorian Britain.* Lewes: Falmer.

SENKER, P. (1986) The Technical and Vocational Education Initiative and economic performance in the United Kingdom: an initial assessment, *Journal of Educational Policy*, 1, 4, 293-303.

SMILES, S. (1986) *Self Help*. Harmondsworth: Penguin.

STRONACH I. *et al* (1982) *Assessment in Youth Training: made-to-measure?* Scottish Vocational Preparation Unit, Jordanhill College, Glasgow.

STRONACH, I. (1984) Work experience: the sacred anvil. In: VARLAMM, C. *Rethinking Transition: educational innovation and the transition to adult life.* Lewes: Falmer.

TURNER, L. W. (1981) *The Drums of Affliction: a study of religious process among the Ndembu of Zambia.* London: International African Institute/ Hutchinson.

WELLENS, J. (1963) *The Training Revolution: from shop-floor to board-room.* London: Evans.

WEINER, J. J. (1981) *English Culture and the Decline in the Industrial Spirit 1850-1980.* Cambridge: Cambridge University Press.

WORSWICK, G. D. N. (ed) (1985) *Education and Economic Performance.* Joint Studies in Public Policy 9. National Institute of Economic and Social Research/Policy Studies Institute/Royal Institute of International Affairs. Aldershot: Gower.

7

Research about Parents in Education

Alastair Macbeth

The spotlight is being turned on parents. To some extent party-political motives seem to be guiding the beam and I do not wish to comment on those. Yet parental involvement is also an *educational* issue of increasing importance and I shall consider what research might be carried out to help to illuminate aspects which at present tend to remain in the penumbral gloom of assumption and assertion.

Although there are exceptions, research into the effects of home background on children's education has tended to be school-centred. It has emphasised school actions and the in-school achievement of pupils, the home elements often assessed by readily-available proxy measures assumed to reflect social class such as paternal occupation, clothing grants and free school meals. This is not surprising for three reasons. The first is that whereas data located in schools and education authorities can be obtained quite readily, the task of getting an acceptable sample of in-home information is time-consuming, expensive and difficult. The second reason is that educational researchers are themselves usually part of the school-oriented establishment. Often trained teachers with previous school experience, they tend to define problems in terms of school functioning. It is not infrequent for them to equate education with institutional provision and to use the words 'school' and 'education' interchangeably. There seems to have been a third reason which may now be diminishing in impetus among researchers but not necessarily among practitioners. This is a tendency to believe that schools can provide the whole of a child's education and even, on their own and unaided by parents, can compensate for disadvantageous backgrounds.

Respected and influential sources have reinforced the flattering confidence in schools' capacity to provide virtually the whole of education. For instance, the 1977 Munn Report stated:

> . . . one of the main functions of schooling is to equip young people with the skills, the knowledge, and the social and moral attitudes which will fit them for full membership of the adult community. (page 15).

Had this been followed by an explanation that parents are integral to the educating process and that a school could only realistically seek such objectives in partnership with them, the claim might have been more credible. 'Outside factors' were briefly acknowledged by Munn and co-operation advocated to 'ensure, as far as possible, that there is no conflict of aims' (page 59), such aims presumably including those quoted above. It was still assumed that schools could achieve those aims. Home environment was seen as 'beyond the school's control' (page 9). Yet assumptions not dissimilar to their statement are still reflected in some Scottish educational circles today.

However, most of a child's education happens outside school in mornings and evenings, at weekends and in school holidays and, of course, in the pre-school years. Indeed, about 85 per cent of a child's waking (and therefore learning) life from birth to 16 years is spent *out* of school. Peer group, local community and media have impact, but much out-of-school learning (especially in the early years) is in-home learning, often deliberate and reinforced by emotional ties of the family and examples set by other members of it. Again and again studies throughout the world have shown a correlation between home background and attainment in school, but too little research has been carried out into the nature of education inside the home and how it can be influenced, in comparison with the volumes devoted to school learning. Since there is evidence of a link between the two, the argument to redress the research balance would seem stronger still. (The multiplicity of studies showing a correlation between home background and school attainment is too extensive and too well-known to warrant listing here. For summaries see Marjoribanks, 1979; Sharrock, 1980; Hewison, 1985; Macbeth, 1987a.) The exact nature of that link remains tantalisingly elusive and, as Rutter *et al* (1979) and Tizard *et al* (1988) show, it should not lead us to underestimate the influence of the school. Clearly both are important.

Assertions, assumptions and philosophies
The field of parental involvement in education is rich in broad assertions but lacks models upon which action can be based. Among the former are the concept of the family as the basic unit of society (though the word 'family' defies clear definition) and parents as the prime educators of their children. Of greater practical significance, most countries place legal responsibility for the education of the individual child on his/her parents, the Scottish reference being section 30 of the Principal Act, currently the Education (Scotland) Act of 1980. Such legal prescription (and associated rights, such as education in accordance with parental wishes) is important in establishing a fundamental point of reference. However laws, being man-made, can be changed. For instance, it would be possible to make

the state (and teachers as its agents) responsible for in-school education, leaving parents with the more limited duty to provide out-of-school education for the child; but that is not so at present and parents are responsible for both. That provides the legal foundation for defining teachers' relations to parents, presumably one of professionals to clients, but it remains a generality.

Various attempts have been made to construct more detailed models. Starting with the over-simple equation of EDUCATION = HOME-LEARNING + SCHOOL-LEARNING + COMMUNITY-LEARNING and then refining it by recognising that each of the three elements interacts with the others and by accepting that all are influenced by a wider culture, a diagram might show three overlapping learning circles representing the home, the school and the community, all set within a rectangle entitled 'Culture'.

Yet this does little more than draw attention to the fact that education is more than mere schooling. Another approach is a modification of the Best *et al* (1983, page 272) inter-linking of three elements of pastoral care which they identify as *education* (academic), *welfare* (pastoral) and *order*

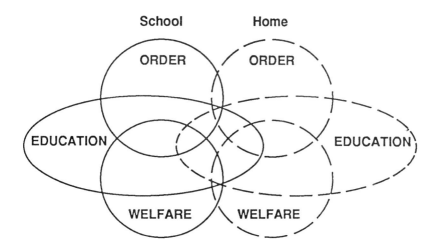

(disciplinary) by which the parallel pastoral care forces in the home can be illustrated as either operating in isolation from the school or in conjunction with it (Macbeth, 1985, page 121).

Long (1986, page 4) has also concentrated on parent-teacher interaction by suggesting that traditionally the primary teacher has been a 'wedge' between parent and child, whereas the more helpful role is as a 'clamp' reinforcing the parent-child learning bond.

However, more sensitive models than these are needed. Some attempts have been made. They seem to fall into two categories: (i) learning-descriptive models, and (ii) policy-prescriptive models. Marjoribanks (1979), among others, has emphasised the complexity of the socio-psychological forces affecting a child's learning. His (1983) model, incorporates personal variables, social status, socio-psychological learning environments and socio-linguistic environments leading to a child's behaviour, but mediated through his/her interpretations of environments.

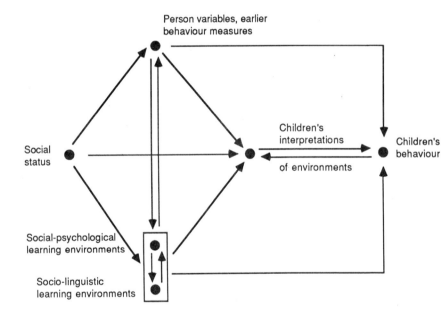

Model for Learning Environment Research

Marjoribanks then relates this model to a family typology distinguishing the levels of parents' aspirations for their child and the extent to which they have dependent/independent-expressive orientations. This is intended as descriptive, does not include the school as such, and illustrates the difficulties of model-building in this field. Schweinhart *et al* (1980, page 65) attempted a causal diagram showing forces upon a child's *school* achievement in which pre-school education, socio-economic status, cognitive ability, commitment to schooling and years of special education were factors in their research. As a causal model it is limited since it does not take into account what forces lead to cognitive ability. Thus, as a minimum, a learning-descriptive model would ideally include all the elements mentioned above, a formidable task.

An interesting alternative approach is one which cuts through the ever more entangled network of socio-psychological influences on a child's learning and seeks to offer a simple model of divided responsibilities between parents and teachers. An Italian parents' organisation (FAES, summarised in Macbeth, 1987b) which, unusually, owns and manages thirteen schools, draws a distinction between the *family-social sphere* of education and the *scholastic sphere,* the latter in effect being the school. Each is said to have *natural factors* (essentially human relations) and *technical factors* (formal teaching). Thus, teaching is recognised as something which happens in the home as well as in the school. This model goes on to assert that each sphere has aspects which are exclusive to parents (natural factors in the home) and exclusive to teachers (technical factors in the school). If the FAES philosophy were converted into Scottish terms it might appear as follows:

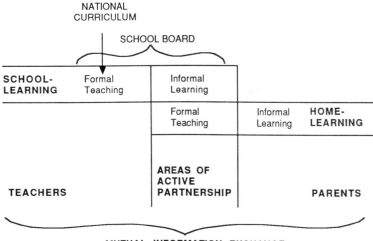

Yet this remains unsatisfactory, for it does not allow for consultative processes, for parental choice within the formally-taught elements of schooling, or for the fact that parents are responsible for the in-school education of their children by law.

I have devoted space to the difficulties of creating models since they highlight the complexity of issues with which we are concerned. Phrases such as 'home-school partnership', 'accountability' and 'parental representation' become confused and uncertain if we cannot state the overall logic of the system of which they are a part. There would seem, therefore, to be a need for both conceptual research and debate to clarify these issues.

Foremost in this process might be a public discussion to determine the proper *educational* (as opposed to party-political) approach to parents in education. The two extremes are to regard parental influence as an evil to be rejected by schools which should compensate energetically, or to view parents as the predominant educators for whom schools provide a supplementing service. The proper course presumably lies somewhere between, but the one view which cannot be sustained any longer is that parents are educationally irrelevant. Yet as Goode (1987, page 108) rightly states:

> a century or so of state education has served to obscure the universally acknowledged truth that a major element of parenting is education.

One of the most passionate adherents to the view that family influence upon education is to be deplored has been Musgrove (1966), but his argument was not based upon the irrelevance of the family, but its impact. 'So successful is the modern conjugal or nuclear family that it is a threat to society' he asserted (page 55) and he argued that it:

> . . . exerts a powerful influence on the prospects, capacity for development, and life-chances of the young. Schools in general are remarkably ineffective in moderating the influence of family background . . . Our contemporary problem is less to buttress the influence of parents than to limit it.

Unfortunately when he comes to what schools should do to provide an antidote to the family, he resorts to vague assertions about the school as an agent of the child and a bridge to the world (without saying in any precise way how), providing specialised skills and knowledge (without saying what they might be) to 'eliminate the influence of parents on the life-chances of the young', and to be a 'corrective of parents'. He calls for teachers to be 'more vigorous, imaginative, aggressive and technically competent', introducing gaiety (a word whose connotations were different in the 1960s) and encouraging achievement that comes from joy.

Such generalised exhortations do not help us to form clear policies, though echoes of his approach can still be encountered in the formal educational system of Scotland today.

If we accept that only about 15 per cent of a child's waking life to age 16 is spent in school, that experience is unlikely to counteract entirely the influence of the 85 per cent outside school. So what approach can schools take? One is to pretend that external influences have no effect or can be remedied by schools. Another is to recognise the school's limitations, but to offer the best facilities possible short of actually attempting to co-operate with parents. Or else schools can view education as a joint home-school process, thereby enabling them to aspire to the objectives of 'educating the whole child' and of equipping young people 'with the skills, the knowledge and the social and moral attitudes which will fit them for full membership of the adult community'. This partnership argument may have more force at pre-school and primary levels than at secondary, but if educational opportunity is to be taken seriously, research must consider the problem at all levels. (For a discussion of the notion of education of the whole child and the parent-teacher relationship as a key element, see FitzHerbert (1985)).

Ideas for research about parents
It is my contention that the place of parents in education has been insufficiently researched, especially in Scotland. The following is a series of ideas which, given resources, researchers might profitably follow up.

(1) Preconceptions about education
In 1979 the Scottish Consumer Council commissioned a survey of a cross-section of Scottish citizens (Atherton, 1979) asking them questions about our education system. Some results were worrying, such as that only about half knew that parents were primarily responsible in law for their child's education, and that more had heard of English governing bodies (43 per cent) than had heard of Scottish school councils (39 per cent). A follow-up study now, a decade later, might pursue some of the same issues for the sake of comparison, but it could range more widely about preconceptions (especially the extent to which education is equated with schooling) and might include questions about recent developments such as the placing request system and school boards. Further, it would be interesting to add samples of teachers, education officers, the Inspectorate and politicians, for it is their preconceptions which determine the nature of the formal system.

(2) Analysis of policy documents
Public documents such as Government statements, reports of committees

and of bodies such as the CCC/SCCC, teachers' unions and the Scottish Parent Teacher Council differ markedly in the extent to which they take into account the parental dimension of education and its management. Analysis of these, followed by interviews with key personnel could tell us much about the forces at work in official circles and why some see parents as educationally relevant while others do not.

(3) Monitoring legislative changes
The 1980's are witnessing important legislative shifts affecting parents and their relationship to schools. Parental choice between schools was confirmed, rather than introduced, by the Education (Scotland) Act of 1981, which also led the way to improved communication between teachers and parents and a greater involvement of parents of children with special educational needs. The Main Report (1986) sought to enhance that relationship further, though it is debatable whether the consolidation of an hours-specific teachers' contract with only limited time devoted to liaison with parents has encouraged or restricted a sense of educational partnership. The School Boards legislation of 1988 will provide parental representation in formal committees but it is unlikely to touch many parents directly in the early years, important though the move could be in managerial terms. Much depends upon what additional legislation is passed once the Boards are established.

Research which monitors, like the University of Glasgow studies on school councils and parental choice (Macbeth, 1980 and University of Glasgow, 1986), might be an appropriate approach, perhaps repeated at intervals and not necessarily carried out by the same institution. A variant of monitoring research, somewhat under-rated in Scotland with its inward-looking traditions, is comparative research; we may have much to learn from countries which are more democratic and educationally open than we are.

(4) Communications between parents and teachers
The past decade has seen the gradual appearance of research into communications between home and school. Bastiani's work, first on written communications (1978) and then on face-to-face contact (1983), was helpful in breaking the ice in Britain, but there is evidence from other countries (e.g. Cornelius *et al*, 1983) that processes in practice can be fraught with tensions, especially in regard to private consultations about the individual child. Work on school reports (Goacher and Reid, 1983), handbooks (Atherton, 1982; Macaulay, 1986) and transition from home to pre-school (Blatchford *et al*, 1982) as well as specialist concerns such as home-school relations in multicultural settings (Tomlinson, 1984) or

for children with learning difficulties (Sandow *et al,* 1987) all deserve increased Scottish attention, as do the impact of the teachers' contract and staffing levels on practice. There is a particular need to look at the question of whether contact between home and school should be a generalist or a specialist function. Do guidance staff and home-school liaison teachers enhance links between teachers and parents, inhibit them by introducing an intermediate bureaucracy, or provide a transitional stage which may dissolve attitudinal barriers and lead to educational collaboration in the future? The *Home from School* investigation of links between homes and the staff of four schools (and supplementary material from 20 others) by John MacBeath and colleagues at Jordanhill College (1986) provides a valuable first step down this road. However much more work starting from differing preconceptions, and dealing with all age groups, is needed. The pastoral care/guidance literature has been especially blinkered in its reluctance to recognise that a constant pastoral care service is provided by families.

(5) Truancy and indiscipline
Since parents bear responsibility for the education of their child and may have marked influence on motivation, a study might be carried out comparing background factors of three categories of pupil: first, those who are persistently truanting and disruptive; secondly, those who conscientiously attend and co-operate but perform poorly in school; thirdly, those who perform well in school. If non-attendance and violence in schools are increasing and are featuring among younger children, work on associated aspects would seem to be relevant. Such work would have to take into account existing evidence about the enduring effect of early childhood learning. However, emphasis should be upon relating beneficial as well as adverse effects to home background.

(6) Parental access to school records
Several countries have legislation allowing parents to see records held on their child in the school or the education authority. In the USA, federal legislation about this was introduced in 1974 on the grounds that it was a question of a civil liberty. States were required to define what should be in an official record and 'No one except a school official or a teacher with a legitimate educational interest may see such records without written consent of the parent.' (Peterson *et al,* 1978, page 331) thereby ensuring that the official record is, indeed, the prime record on the child. Parents have the right not only to see that record but to challenge judgements recorded on it. English legislation will have a similar effect.

In Scotland, a study could usefully be mounted to look at what information is held on pupils by schools and education authorities (on both official and unofficial records), the extent to which parents have access to those records, are encouraged in this and are informed (e.g. at regular private consultations) of changes. Variations of practice between education authorities might be revealing. Modes of reporting to outside bodies (e.g. potential employers, other schools) about pupils and the extent to which judgements and facts included in such reports are available to the child's parents could be included.

(7) PAs and PTAs
Little research has been done into the roles, actual and potential, of parents' associations and parent-teacher associations, but such bodies ought to increase in importance as support mechanisms to the new school boards. Their image has generally been bad on both sides of the Atlantic because they have accepted an educationally peripheral role, but Continental European experience suggests that this could change. A Scottish study such as Nias (1981) carried out in England might be a starting point.

(8) The Micropolitics of home-school relations
Micropolitics has been defined by Hoyle (1982, page 88) as 'those strategies by which individuals and groups in organisational contexts seek to use their resources of power and influence to further their interests'. One only has to observe a school with an active and perceptive parent body and a headteacher who regards all school matters as his professional domain to recognise that the micropolitics of home-school relations could be a spicy topic to study. The reverse is often true, that a head (or other staff), anxious to involve parents to a greater extent, finds resistance from those parents. Case studies of strategies, successes and failures in diverse types of schools could be valuable.

(9) Homework
A recent DES Inspectorate report (1987, page 44) asserts that homework is 'important for pupils of all ages and abilities'; Rutter *et al* (1979, page 109) reported that secondary schools which set homework frequently and checked on whether staff did in fact set it, tended to have better outcomes than schools which did not; the White Paper *Better Schools* (1985, page 25) referred to homework as an important element of study; and there is growing evidence that home assistance to young children with reading is valuable. In *Homework in Europe* (Macbeth, 1987(c), pages 4-7), I attempted to bring together not only the purposes for homework which were seen as acceptable and questionable in various European countries,

but also eleven features which were perceived as integral to effective homework. However there seems to have been little systematic research into homework and those eleven features might provide a framework for it.

(10) Home-learning
We may draw a distinction between homework and home-learning:

Homework: Learning tasks set by teachers to be completed out of class (normally in the home) within a specified time and usually directly related to work currently being done at school.

Home-learning: All learning which happens in the home as a result of family actions. It may or may not be deliberate; it may or may not be beneficial; and it includes knowledge, skills, attitudes and habits acquired by emulation as well as instruction.

(Macbeth, forthcoming, 1989)

Here we are approaching much more central educational issues than appeared in the first eight suggestions above. If children from certain kinds of homes achieve better than those from others, then concerns for equality of opportunity, best use of talent and almost any other educational objective would need to take home-learning into account. Although it may be beyond our control, it need not be beyond our influence and still less beyond our capacity to carry out research into it.

Tizard and Hughes (1984, pages 250-252), who looked at the home-learning of four-year-olds, suggested that there are five reasons why the home is an especially effective learning environment for the young child. The range of activities is greater than in school, there is reference to the existing framework of knowledge, there is more personal attention, the context is of significance and the parent-child bond is close. However, they recognised that there are difficulties in carrying out such research. Not only does it involve intrusion into homes, likely distortion of events through the researcher's presence, and expense in time and money in doing such research, but they suggest that there is 'the belief in some quarters that there is not much to be gained from attempting to do so . . . the general belief that mothers, as educators, have very little to offer.'

Hewison (1985) whose own work suggests that parents' assistance was a strong factor in children's reading ability, quite properly cautions against extravagant claims for home-learning and the assumption that a process which assists six-year olds also applies to other children (page 57). The recent report *Young Children at School in the Inner City* by Tizard *et al* (1988) emphasises the complexity of home-school learning interactions, and it reminds us of how research findings can conflict and how much remains to be ascertained. Yet there does seem to be enough evidence about the relationship between home-learning and school-learning to warrant research into the former as much as the latter. To date, British studies of home-learning have tended to concentrate on very young children (e.g. Tizard and Hughes, 1984; Davie *et al,* 1984) and work might be extended over the age range.

(11) Who influences types of learning?

It may be hypothesised that a child would learn most about quadratic equations from school, current natural disasters from television, the practice of sex from peers and many social attitudes from the family. Teachers and parents may seek to teach him about all four, but, in terms of impact, these sources of learning probably differ in their effectiveness. Current debates about whether television influences attitudes to sex and violence underline not only how little we know about the socio-psychological factors at work but how difficult it is to get to know.

It might be valuable to separate out the elements of a child's learning and assess these relative influences of school, peer-groups, family, local community and media at different age levels. There is not space to elaborate here, but certain forms of cognitive learning traditionally associated with the school curriculum might be distinguished from civic competence and social and moral attitudes, for instance. Inevitably multiple sources of learning will affect each element. The Danish organisation *Skole og Samfund* (school and society) has a game played by teachers and parents in which specific skills or knowledge of a young person (ability to swim 200 metres; names of the planets; highway code; etc) are analysed in terms of which adults should ensure the attainment of that competence if it is deemed appropriate. Repeatedly the conclusion is that learning must be in both home and school, but sometimes more one than the other. It is the nature of this division of impact which initially deserves research. The results could assist schools not only to see where their efforts are most effective, but in which aspects of education they should collaborate most closely with parents as co-educators.

Conclusion

We have *education* authorities, a Scottish *Education* Department, a Scottish Council for Research in *Education*, and a range of other formal bodies with official concern for education. Yet the emphasis is almost always on institutional provision (especially schools) rather than on education in a broader sense. If the welfare of children is the concern of these bodies, then there would seem to be good grounds for taking more seriously the non-institutional educational forces. A new research emphasis could be the first step.

Note
Permission from K. Marjoribanks to use the model shown on page 27 is gratefully acknowledged.

References
ATHERTON, G. (1979) *Reaching Out to Parents: an exploratory study of parents and schooling in Scotland.* Glasgow: Scottish Consumer Council.
ATHERTON, G. (1982) *The Book of the School.* Glasgow: Scottish Consumer Council.
BASTIANI, J. (1978) *Written Communication Between Home and School.* University of Nottingham.
BASTIANI, J. (ed) (1983) *Teacher/Parent Interviews: some materials for teachers.* University of Nottingham School of Education.
BEST, R., RIBBINS, P.M., JARVIS, C. and ODDY, D. (1983) *Education and Care.* London: Heinemann Educational Books.
BLATCHFORD, P., BATTLE, S.*and* MAYS, J. (1982) *The First Transition: home to pre-school.* Windsor: NFER-Nelson.
CORNELIUS, H., RAVN, B. *and* BINGER, B. (1983) *Focus on Family — School Communications: a Danish approach.* Advance paper for EEC School and Family Conference, Luxembourg.
DAVIE, C. E., HUTT, S. J., VINCENT, E. *and* MASON, M. (1984) *The Young Child at Home.* Windsor: NFER-Nelson.
DEPARTMENT OF EDUCATION AND SCIENCE (1985) *Better Schools.* White Paper. London: H.M.S.O.
DEPARTMENT OF EDUCATION AND SCIENCE (1987) *Homework: a report by HM Inspectors.* London: DES.
EDUCATION (SCOTLAND) ACT, 1980, 44. Edinburgh: H.M.S.O.
EDUCATION (SCOTLAND) ACT, 1981, 58. Edinburgh: H.M.S.O.
FITZHERBERT, K. (1985) Parents, teachers and the 'whole child', pp 97-116. In: CULLINGFORD, C. (ed), *Parents, Teachers and Schools.* Robert Bryce.
GOACHER, B. *and* REID, M. I. (1983) *School Reports to Parents.* Windsor: NFER-Nelson.
GOODE, J. (1987) Parents as Educators, pp 108-124. In: BASTIANI (ed), *Parents and Teachers 1.* Windsor: NFER-Nelson.
HEWISON, (1985) The evidence of case studies of parents' involvement in schools, 3. In: CULLINGFORD, C. (ed) *Parents, Teachers and Schools.* Robert Bryce.
HOYLE, E. (1982) Micropolitics of educational organizations. In: *Educational Management and Administration,* 10, 87-88.
LONG, R. (1986) *Developing Parental Involvement in Primary Schools.* London: MacMillan Education.

MACAULAY, C. (1986) Information for Parents, 5. In: UNIVERSITY OF GLASGOW. *Parental Choice of School in Scotland.* Parental Choice Project. University of Glasgow, Department of Education.

MACBEATH, J. MEARNS, D. *and* SMITH M. (1986) *Home from School.* Jordanhill College of Education, Department of Education.

MACBETH, A. M., MACKENZIE, M. L. *and* BRECKENRIDGE, I. (1980) *Scottish School Councils: policy-making, participation or irrelevance?* Edinburgh: H.M.S.O.

MACBETH, A. M. (1985) Parents, Schools and Pastoral Care: some research priorities, pp 114-129. In: LANG, P. *and* MARYLAND, M. *New Directions in Pastoral Care.* Oxford: Blackwell.

MACBETH, A. M. (1987a) *Some British Research Studies into the Relationship between Pupils' Home Backgrounds and In-School Attainment.* University of Glasgow, Home and School Study Unit 4.

MACBETH, A. M. (1987b) *Home-Learning in Childhood.* University of Glasgow, Home and School Study Unit 5.

MACBETH, A. M. (1987c), *Homework in Europe.* European Parents' Association.

MACBETH, A. M. (1989 forthcoming) *Involving Parents.* London: Heinemann.

MAIN COMMITTEE (1986) *Committee of Inquiry Report into the Pay and Conditions of Service of School Teachers in Scotland.* Cmnd 9893. (The Main Report). Edinburgh: H.M.S.O.

MARJORIBANKS, K. (1979) *Families and their Learning Environments: an empirical analysis.* London: Routledge and Kegan Paul.

MARJORIBANKS, K. (1983) *Family Learning Environments: an overview.* Advance paper to the EEC School and Family Conference, Luxembourg.

MUSGROVE, F. (1966) *The Family, Education and Society.* London: Routledge and Kegan Paul.

NIAS, J. (1981) Parent Associations, 8. In: ELLIOTT, J., BRIDGES, D., EBBUTT, D., GIBSON, R. *and* NIAS, J. *School Accountability.* London: Grant McIntyre.

PETERSON, L. J., ROSSMILLER, R. A. *and* VOLZ, M. M. (1978) *The Law and Public School Operation,* 2nd edition, London: Harper and Row.

RUTTER, M., MAUGHAN, B., MORTIMORE, P. *and* OUSTON, J. (1979) *Fifteen Thousand Hours: secondary schools and their effects on children.* Somerset: Open Books.

SANDOW, S., STAFFORD, D. *and* STAFFORD, P. (1987) *An Agreed Understanding? Parent-Professional Communication and the 1981 Act.* Windsor: NFER-Nelson.

SCHWEINHART, L. J. *and* WEIKART, D. P. (1980) *Young Children Grow Up: the effects of the Perry Preschool Program on youths through age 15.* Michigan: High/Scope.

SCOTTISH EDUCATION DEPARTMENT (1977) *The Structure of the Curriculum in the Third and Fourth Years of the Scottish Secondary School.* (Munn Report). Edinburgh: H.M.S.O.

SHARROCK, A. (1980) Research on Home-School Relations, 6. In: CRAFT,

M., RAYNOR, J. *and* COHEN, L. (eds) *Linking Home and School,* (3rd edition). London: Harper and Row.

TIZARD, B. *and* HUGHES, M. (1984) *Young Children Learning: talking and thinking at home and at school.* Fontana Original.

TIZARD, B., BLATCHFORD, P., BURKE, J., FARQUHAR, C. *and* PLEWIS, I. (1988) *Young Children at School in the Inner City.* Sussex: Lawrence Erlbaum Associates.

TOMLINSON, S. (1984) *Home and School in Multicultural Britain: education in a multicultural society.* London: Batsford.

UNIVERSITY OF GLASGOW (1986) *Parental Choice of School in Scotland.* Parental Choice Project. University of Glasgow, Department of Education.

8

Resource-Based Teaching: the New Pedagogy?

Eric Drever

Scottish secondary schools have undergone profound changes during the last quarter of a century. During the 1960s they 'went comprehensive' at a pace unmatched elsewhere in the UK. The 1970s saw the raising of the leaving age from 15 to 16, with consequent pressure to reform or replace the 'O' Grade examination, designed for an academic minority, and to provide a national certificate for all at the end of compulsory schooling. The response was the setting up in 1975 of the Munn and Dunning committees to review respectively the curriculum (1977b), and assessment and certification (1977a), for the 14-16 age group. Some of the far-reaching developments that followed are described in Brown and Munn (1985); the work is still far from over. It can be argued that only now are Scottish secondary schools beginning to implement the kind of curriculum and assessment that was implicit in the organisational reforms of previous decades. However, Munn and Dunning were not matched by any comparable report on teaching. Various curriculum documents stress that teachers will need in-service training to develop new skills, but the skills are ill-defined add-on extras, with no discussion of the skills teachers are supposed to have already and how these might be developed. There is no single clear statement of a desired post-Munn-and-Dunning pedagogy.

The trend towards resource-based learning

Over the period discussed, there has been a trend towards individualised and resource-based learning, as a way of dealing with the increasingly diverse range of abilities and motivation likely to be found in a typical class at any stage of secondary education. By now most subjects have materials for first and second year mixed-ability classes that allow pupils a measure of self-paced learning and differentiation of tasks according to previous progress. With the introduction of Standard Grade courses for the 14-16 age group it is possible that resource-based activities will displace the teacher-led lesson as the norm of pupils' secondary school experience. This trend gains support from a number of ideas put into circulation by the Munn and Dunning reports, or during the subsequent developments. Some of these ideas concern the curriculum. For example there has been emphasis on *relevance*: pupils should find and apply 'real' knowledge to realistic problems. Standard Grade curricula play down *content* in favour of *skills* and *products* in favour of *processes*. In such cases, a pedagogy based on learning activities seems more appropriate than the teacher-centred delivery of lessons.

Other ideas relate to learning and the learner. A constructivist view, that pupils 'make sense' of our teaching using their existing ideas and ways of thinking, suggests that we should try to 'go with the grain' of pupils' mental activity and not simply impose our alien ideas. The traditional view of ability has also been challenged by Bloom's notion that it is an 'alterable variable' (Bloom, 1976) and courses now include diagnosis-and-remediation cycles, as a first step towards an individualised mastery learning strategy.

These ideas often circulate in half-baked forms, and though they help sway people towards adopting a resource-based approach, there is no guarantee that the resulting courses will be founded on the ideas. Indeed the most powerful pressures towards embracing a resource-based strategy may be practical organisational considerations. Few schools will be able to offer a proper range of Standard Grade courses at all three Levels (Foundation, General and Credit) unless they create classes which are not only *mixed-ability* but *multi-Level,* with pupils studying the same subject but different topics, or the same topics at different levels, or at different rates.

The possibility of schools introducing resource-based learning as a way of coping with multi-Level classes in Standard Grade, led in 1984 to an evaluation study of the existing resource-based programme 'Choice Chemistry'. This was the brainchild of three chemistry teachers in Lothian Region. They aimed to cater for 70 per cent of the ability range, presenting the more able for Scottish 'O' Grade and the others for a CSE certificate of the Northern Region Examination Board. While the course had many features found in other resource-based schemes (and in subsequent Standard Grade developments) it was an unusually comprehensive package, and extended secondments allowed the authors to provide exemplary in-service support. The research was immediately concerned with the effectiveness of this programme, and the demands and benefits experienced by teachers and learners; more speculatively, it considered resource-based methods in general as a way of coping with the post-Munn curriculum. More fundamentally it was intererested in whether resource-based methods would be found to reflect or bring about a change in thinking, incorporating the kinds of ideas discussed earlier; and whether there would be a shift in curricular control from the teacher towards the learner, over, say, the definition of knowledge, access to learning, and the validation and accreditation of attainment.

Features of resource-based learning

There is an extensive professional literature which argues the case for individualised and resource-based methods, and gives valuable practical advice on the design and organisation of materials and programmes. Much of this writing is propagandist, contrasting the 'rigid lock-step teacher-dominated' traditional classroom with 'pupil-centred' learning in which learners are 'free to explore materials to the limits of their abilities and interests'. Such stereotypes do not reflect the observable variety and complexity within both traditional and resource-based practices, and the ambivalent logic and subtle balancing of priorities that lies behind the behaviour that we observe. As with Standard Grade plans, the writers often concede that these approaches make new demands on teachers' and learners' skills and attitudes, but there is little discussion of what they will do, and say to each other; there is little cross-reference to research on teachers' thinking; and generally writers seem trapped within an objectives-based 'systems' approach, which may be useful in relation to programme design, but whose relevance to classroom pedagogy is remote.

The extent of individualisation in a programme can be judged by asking: who has control, and over what? Most schemes offer the learner little choice of *what* is to be learned, or *how* (the methods and media to be used). Choice Chemistry offers different *levels* of study (its different 'extension' tasks), but the main element of learner control is the *self-pacing* of work. Both teachers and pupils mentioned this as the single most important difference between the resource-based and traditional approaches, and on occasions explicitly connected it with a notion of 'mastery': 'pupils have time to master the work before moving on'; 'you have time to understand'. The extent to which self-pacing is realised in practice, and the way in which time is used, are important in understanding the possible benefits of resource-based methods, and we shall discuss these further.

Claims for resource-based learning

The literature suggests four main types of claim for resource-based and individualised strategies, which we tested against our evidence about Choice Chemistry.

The first simply asserts that students have the right to direct their own learning. The authors of Choice Chemistry certainly believed in this, and the pupils, more than anything else about the course, valued the sense of independence it gave them.

The second rather fatalistic claim, common in writing for teachers, is that if mixed-ability classes are inevitable, resource-based methods allow teachers and pupils to cope. They lead to reduced frustration for the most- and least-able pupils, good teacher/pupil working relationships, less stress and discipline problems, and so, better conditions for working and learning. The Choice Chemistry teachers endorsed most of these claims.

A third claim, that resource-based methods improve cognitive learning, is conspicuous by its absence, given the emphasis in secondary curricula and examinations on this type of learning. UK and Scottish evidence is sparse and equivocal, and a major review (Bangert 1983) found disappointing results in America. Analysis of 'O' Grade scripts made available by the Scottish Examination Board in 1985 showed that Choice Chemistry students' results were relatively poorer.

Finally, it may be claimed that resource-based methods are the route to new kinds of learning: skills, processes, attitudes. Little is said in the literature about how these are to be fostered, or about retention and transfer, and again Bangert found scant evidence of improvement in these areas (*op cit*). There was some evidence that Choice Chemistry improved pupils' writing skills. However the most striking contrast with traditional schools lay in the pupils' attitudes to the course and the subject.

Structured questionnaires showed that in 'traditional' schools, pupils' reactions varied with the teacher, but chemistry was generally seen as difficult and boring. Only occasionally did enjoyment match the level typical of Choice Chemistry schools, where the course was seen as easy to follow and interesting (even when the teacher was described as boring!). The features students enjoyed, and saw as characteristic of Choice Chemistry were:

— 'doing experiments'
— 'working on your own' (i.e. 'not just listening to the teacher' 'without the teacher standing over you')
— 'working at your own pace'
— 'writing up your own notes'

The two pedagogies
The resource-based approach can create a learning environment that is popular with teacher and pupil, and perceived as quite different from the traditional classroom. Self-pacing is a key element. But it does amount to a new pedagogy, reflecting new ideas about knowledge, teaching and learning and a real shift in control over the curriculum? We need to look more closely at the two approaches.

'Traditional teaching'
Traditional teaching is not pure lecturing. Different subjects have their various characteristic modes of activity involving teacher and learner.

The literature on teachers' thinking suggests that they carry in mind a variety of 'scenarios' of the productive classroom, corresponding to these various modes. Lessons are planned as sequences of episodes based on these scenarios, and class teaching depends on routines for bringing into play the appropriate sets of rules to maintain the current scenario or switch to a new one for the next segment of the lesson.

Within each mode the teacher will somehow combine instructional interaction with individuals and the management of class activity as a whole. This is especially demanding in teacher-centred episodes and teachers develop various tactics: using pseudo-questions to move the lesson on, or quell inattention; ensuring that they get the answer they want by asking pupils who are expected to know, asking several pupils, re-phrasing half-right answers, and so on.

Whole class teaching can thus be immensely skilful, yet not be very effective as instruction. In both traditional and Choice Chemistry classes, pupils reported how immensely difficult it was to follow teacher-led lessons. Often teachers went too fast, or the lesson got bogged down and repetitive: but if you missed a single point you might be lost from there on. By comparison, in resource-based work, you could stop and think, or even drift off, without losing track.

Science lessons traditionally involve teacher-centred episodes and practical work by pupils, and often have three main segments. In the first the teacher establishes what is to be investigated and gives instructions for the 'experiment'; then the pupils work in pairs with the teacher supervising; and finally the teacher gathers the results, these are discussed, and some notes written. If the aim of *teaching* is to *establish understanding and consolidate knowledge* then in the first segment some teaching will certainly be occurring; however much of the time will be spent in setting the scene, reminding pupils of previous work, and giving instructions. Besides, the teaching will be diluted by the need to manage the class and maintain pupils' attention. In the middle segment there is scope for teaching as the teacher moves around the class, but often teachers concentrate instead on ensuring that the 'experiments' work, and give a 'good' set of results, deliberately postponing most of the real teaching until the discussion in the final segment, when again it will be diluted by the need to handle the whole class. Thus the efficiency of the process, measured as the ratio of *effective teaching* to *total time taken* may not be high.

The resource-based approach

The resource-based strategy implies various differences in pedagogy. For one thing, lesson planning, in the traditional sense of planning to cover a particular topic and have the class achieve specific learning outcomes during the lesson period, largely disappears. Instead teachers have to become knowledgeable about the whole of the current unit, and be broadly aware of the stages reached by the individual pupils. There will be one predominant mode of activity, in which the teacher circulates in a supervisory role as well as interacting with groups and individuals.

Despite what some writers seem to imply, the aim of the programmes such as Choice Chemistry is not 'to release teachers from teaching' so that they spend their time managing resources and activities. It is to release them *for* teaching:

> . . .the teacher is removed from the control and directive role in teaching, to an interactive role. The learning materials were meant to stand up on their own so that the teacher was freed from low-level management and organizational tasks . . . to high level personal associations with students.
>
> (Interview with one Choice Chemistry author)

Teachers using the course endorsed this view. They referred to the materials as guiding the pupils' *work*, but not as the source of *learning*. They and the pupils still saw this as dependent on the teachers' actions.

In the Choice Chemistry equivalent of the lesson described previously, the instructions would be given by the work-cards; discussion of results would be by pupils working in pairs; the writing up would be the responsibility of the learner. The pattern of activity throughout would be rather like the 'experiment' section of the traditional lesson, except that the teacher would not simply supervise but would intervene to supplement what pupils gained from the work-cards and learning activities. Thus the whole of the lesson time would become available for 'teaching'. But that time must now be divided amongst perhaps ten groups of learners, giving six to eight minutes per group per lesson: not a lot of teaching! Of course we can expect the time to be spent more effectively because the teacher can concentrate on what is relevant to each group in turn, can question individual pupils closely, and can expect to get their full attention. But if resource-based teaching is to improve the ratio of *effective teaching* to *total time taken* then teachers need to be very disciplined and economical in the management of their own time: they must make contact when pupils most need it; during contact they must give priority to what the work-cards or the pupils themselves cannot deal with.

The teachers' view

The teachers' view of the resource-based approach was very much as we have suggested. The main benefit the majority claimed was the satisfaction from helping pupils learn during one-to-one contact. They emphasised how hard they had to work to keep track of the activities and be available to pupils when they needed help. The second benefit they claimed was in the improved motivation and involvement of the pupils. Though the classroom was now busier and noisier, it was on balance less stressful for both teacher and pupil, providing better conditions for teaching, and so, for learning.

These benefits arise because there is no longer the pressure involved in maintaining the attention of the whole class, including those who already understand or are already lost. Instructional interaction need not be compromised and interrupted by other things, and teacher and pupil need not lose the thread. A more profound potential benefit is that teaching need no longer be a matter of presenting a lesson that is only approximately matched to the previous learning and interests of any one pupil, and cannot adjust to their individual state of 'readiness' at a particular moment. In principle, resource-based teaching could aim to create conditions in which mastery could be achieved and retained.

The observer's view

Time is used differently in traditional and resource-based pedagogies. The first places a premium on planning and controlling pupils' progress through a series of episodes. The second emphasises the management of teachers' time in co-ordinating a set of resource-based teaching routines. The teachers were aware of having exchanged one of these pressures for the other. But had they developed the routines needed to exploit the new approach? Our classroom observation suggested that they were mostly simply 'taking the teaching round the room'. (Of course a lot had been achieved in simply clearing the ground: the organisation of resources, the training of pupils to use them responsibly and accept the regime of working, discussing and writing up without the teacher's immediate presence.)

One resource-based routine is 'circuiting' in which the teacher goes round the class making social contact and gaining an overview of progress, but without 'teaching'. The authors of Choice Chemistry saw an initial circuit as very important: teachers should use it to find out who is going to need help and then plan their resource-based teaching for the rest of the period. Most teachers did not attempt this and tended simply to respond to events.

During resource-based lessons two main teaching activities were observed which we call 'checkpointing' and 'trouble-shooting'. Resource-based materials often include 'checkpoints' when pupils should show their work to the teacher. Around this develops the routine of 'checkpointing': those occasions when teachers mark jotters and discuss individual pupils' recent work with them in some detail. Choice Chemistry teachers saw this as a main opportunity for resource-based teaching: for assisting and assessing pupils' learning. Despite the clear advice given by the authors, checkpointing was handled in a variety of ways. In some classes it was initiated by pupils when they finished a task. This could lead to queues, or to pupils marking time on other activities. In other classes teachers checkpointed pupils in turn, irrespective of the stage they had reached, and some might in the meantime have developed a back-log of mistakes and problems. 'Troubleshooting', when pupils approach the teacher for help in understanding, or in carrying out or interpreting the experiments or writing tasks, might be integrated with pupil-initiated checkpointing, or might be separate, and sometimes interrupted other teaching routines.

One conclusion from our observation is that resource-based materials do not impose uniformity of practice (which some teachers feared). Teachers' personal views about resource-based learning, their own responsibilities, the capabilities of their pupils and so on, are reflected in their classroom priorities. Some accept responsibility for ensuring that learning occurs, others only for checking whether it has occurred, or that activities have been completed. Some share control of the learning, and let pupils assess themselves and choose the extensions they will try. Some pester the pupils for homework, others leave them to be responsible for this aspect of learning.

Again if, as teachers believe, teacher/pupil contacts are a main factor bringing about learning, then resource-based pedagogy does not guarantee equality of opportunity to learn. Some pupils had more contact than others, or different kinds of contact, depending on the teachers' perception of their ability or trouble-making potential, or their own willingness to approach the particular teacher.

If this seems similar to traditional classrooms, then so was the teacher/ pupil dialogue. In checkpointing, teachers did the majority of the talking, and there were long passages peppered with questions requiring only brief student responses. Correct written work was by implication taken as evidence of learning, and discussion centred on mistakes and difficulties. Rather than exploring the reasoning pupils had used, teachers led them through the reasoning they should have used, and there was often heavy prompting that 'homed pupils in' on the correct answer. Sometimes they were simply given the answer, with or without explanation. Thus while the tone was usually pleasant, the exchanges were teacher-dominated, and the emphasis was on the negative. One reason for this is that teachers are not present during the activities or discussions with partners when initial learning takes place. As a result, teacher/pupil talk is retrospective and remedial. To implement the ideas mentioned earlier or create conditions for 'mastery' other routines would need to be developed: routines of Pre-emptive teaching aiming to ensure that pupils will carry out tasks correctly; attend to important aspects; and have the skills, knowledge and ideas needed to learn from the task; routines for diagnosing specific misunderstandings or more general difficulties; routines for counselling about longer-term learning or skill development.

Conclusions

The authors of Choice of Chemistry were aware of severe constraints: the 'O' Grade syllabus and examinations which were not designed to exploit and reward resource-based methods; the inadequate time allocation for the course. They were aware of compromising, with conventional views of the curriculum and of teaching. Similar constraints and compromises are likely to beset any development of resource-based programmes within Standard Grade, and if we are to transform pedagogy positively rather than just giving teachers a coping strategy, then we need to tackle a number of issues.

The problem of time

A main reason why a more elaborated resource-based pedagogy had not developed was the shortage of time within the programme. Of course, teachers always say they have not enough time, but the literature is fairly consistent in suggesting that resource-based or mastery learning programmes take about 20 per cent longer than traditional methods. And time appears critical. With conventional instruction, teachers can cut corners and speed up to fit the time available. In individualised working, that may undermine the whole approach, preventing proper self-pacing, cutting off learning before mastery is achieved, and causing teachers to restrict their resource-based teaching to a minimal range of routines. Choice Chemistry certainly suffered from this.

The design of materials

An evaluation of the resource-based ASEP programme (Tisher and Power 1975, 1978) offered two interesting conclusions: that teachers' skills and attitudes strongly influenced the success of the programme; and that we know very little about how to design learning materials or how pupils interact with them. Resource materials should not be bits of teaching put on paper and made teacher- and pupil- proof. The teachers should be more than mere checkpointers. Choice Chemistry certainly aimed at something more. If it is the *combination* of materials-based activities and resource-based teaching that leads to the most effective learning, then we need to study how materials can be designed to set up fruitful contacts between pupils, resources and teachers.

The nature of learning activities

Different subjects have their traditional 'learning activities'. In science it is 'doing experiments'. White and Tisher (1986) question this 'matter of dogma'. Research evidence (including ours) shows that practical work is popular, but that learners may simply 'go through the motions' of one activity after another. The most promising results seem to depend on students being genuinely involved in investigations over which they have some real control, but this is hardly the case with most of the worksheet tasks we find in science classes. We should not assume that activities developed as an adjunct of teaching can form the staple of learning.

The structure of the subject

Proponents of resource-based learning seem addicted to the instructional objectives model, in which subjects become collections of individually trivial behavioural outcomes (in the case of Choice Chemistry, about 900). There is a danger that coherence in learning is lost, and with it, retention: they do it, check it, forget it. One strength of traditional teaching, overlooked in the naive fashion for disparaging 'content', is that the teachers' own grasp of the framework provided by the subject can create coherence across lessons and topics. Resource-based programmes too often leave coherence to the learner.

References

BANGERT, R., KULIK, J. A. *and* KULIK, C. C. (1983) Individualized systems of instruction in secondary schools, *Review of Educational Research*, 53, 2.

BLOOM, B. (1976) *Human Characteristics and School Learning*. New York: McGraw-Hill.

BROWN, S. *and* MUNN, P. (eds) (1985) *The Changing Face of Education 14 to 16: curriculum and assessment*. Windsor: NFER-Nelson.

SCOTTISH EDUCATION DEPARTMENT (1977a) *Assessment for All: report of the committee to review assessment in the third and fourth years of secondary education in Scotland*. (The Dunning Report). Edinburgh: HMSO.

SCOTTISH EDUCATION DEPARTMENT (1977b) *The Structure of the Curriculum in the Third and Fourth Years of the Scottish Secondary School*. (The Munn Report). Edinburgh: HMSO.

TISHER, R. *and* POWER, C. (1975) A study of the effects of teaching strategies in ASEP classrooms, *Australian Journal of Education*, 19, 2.

TISHER, R. *and* POWER, C. (1978) The learning environment associated with an Australian curriculum innovation, *Journal of Curriculum Studies,* 10, 2.

WHITE, R. *and* TISHER, R. (1986) Research on teaching in the natural sciences, Chapter 30. In: WITTROCK, M. (ed) *Handbook of Research on Teaching (Third edition).* New York: AERA/Macmillan.

9

Radical Pedagogy for Conservative Schooling?
14-18 in Scotland

David Hartley

Opportunities for less well-qualified pupils, already decimated by the reduction in semi-skilled jobs, are further eroded. Fundamentally, education and careers education in particular must face questions such as: is the traditional work ethic still relevant; is job satisfaction still a priority or is any job, in fact, better than none? (CCC, 1986a, page 26)

There is an emerging social category in educational discourse: 'young people', normally of less-than-average ability and aged between 14 and 18. This group straddles the school/college divide, even though it is being regarded as homogeneous in respect of its needs. This paper argues, speculatively, that there is an emerging institutional educational structure for 'young people' of this type. If implemented, it would do much to undermine the ideal that the comprehensive (or 'omnibus') school is 'the natural way for a democracy to order the post-primary schooling of a given area' (SED, 1947). The position taken here is that the Standard Grade course *Social and Vocational Skills (SVS)* and the 16+ programme *Personal and Social Development (PSD)* constitute the curricular catalysts of this new provision. The analysis is set within contemporary economic policy.

During the early stages of the Industrial Revolution, factory-based production required both a new organisational structure for the workplace and a new set of attitudes to time, space and discipline on the part of the worker (Pollard, 1965; O'Neill, 1986). A technical process which divided the production process was best served by a bureaucratic form of organisation, perhaps exemplified by F. W. Taylor's 'scientific management' approach. In order to facilitate the worker's transition into the bureaucratised setting, there was a need to prepare him or her psychologically for it, and thus the curriculum of mass elementary schooling, introduced in the 1870s, gave explicit attention to what would now be called social and vocational skills (Vallance, 1973).

Since then, bureaucracy has burgeoned to such an extent that Berger *et al* (1973) refer to the 'bureaucratic cognitive style' as becoming the dominant mode of consciousness in modern industrial society. Among the elements of this style are: to consider parts, not wholes; to homogenise, standardise and rationalise; to produce tables, lists and taxonomies; to be concerned with predictability, not creativity; to monitor, test and evaluate. But there are limits to the pure bureaucratic control advocated by the scientific management school. The limits were breached in the USA during the 1920s, and a new, 'softer' form of bureaucracy, developed by industrial psychologists, was introduced by management. This human relations management theory 'loosens' (Bidwell, 1965) the bureaucratic form. It regards the worker as a psychological entity whose perceived social and psychological needs should be catered for, but only insofar as they accord with the formal goals of management. In this looser structure, compliance increasingly results from self-control or from collegial control, not from hierarchical control. The proponents of human relations management tend to use terms which are becoming common coin in the managerial jargon of the SED: *participation, consultation* and *negotiation*. These procedures, of course, require a good measure of communication and social skills on the part of worker and manager alike. Moreover, as the economy shifts away from manufacturing to the provision of services, so these communication skills will become increasingly necessary. Thus, from the standpoint of employers, a human relations approach to classroom management would be appropriate for two reasons: first, it would anticipate the managerial regime of the service sector; second, it would provide the pupil with the social skills required by that sector. This emphasis on general demeanour is reflected in the wishes of employers: that is, whilst they are a little vague about the *specific* skills required of the school-leaver, they are agreed that he should have the 'right attitude' to work (Wellington, 1986).

Apart from the earliest years of mass schooling, the inculcation of attitudes has been the remit of the hidden curriculum. In post-primary education, this curriculum has tacitly transmitted what Berger calls the 'bureaucratic cognitive style'. But this hidden curriculum is not universally acceptable to pupils, and — more to the point — it will be discordant with the adult lives many will face: that is, a life where change is the norm (Stonier, 1979). Already there are groups in society, such as the young unemployed, whose school-based hidden curriculum has ill-prepared them for their marginality to the wage economy. [In 1983, youth unemployment for those under twenty was 25.7 per cent (Marsden, 1986).] Plunkett (1982) has defined these groups as 'risk groups' in the sense that they are economically and socially disadvantaged. Increasingly, they become marginal to society's institutions.

For the low-achieving 14-18 year-old, the hidden curriculum is in flux. In Scotland, two points mark this. First, at the level of policy, the SED have advocated for post-primary education a progressivist pedagogy which has similarities with that recommended in the Primary Memorandum (SED, 1965; Hartley, 1987). Exposure to this new pedagogy, so the argument goes, would foster flexibility, self-motivation and self-reliance in the young person. These 'qualities' would have a dual function: they would provide the communication and social skills for the emerging service sector; they would foster self-reliance in those unemployed. This constitutes what is termed here as an instrumentalisation of the expressive order of the school. To develop this point: there have been very urgent moves to formalise the content of the hidden curriculum — to make it manifest (Hartley, 1985). The evidence for this lies in the Standard Grade course *Social and Vocational Skills*, and in the 16+ course *Personal and Social Development* (SEB, 1984; SED, 1985). Both courses provide social education, but it should be noted that they have been undertaken *separately* in secondary and in further education. Nevertheless, the argument here is that, so close are their respective endeavours, that they comprise an articulation, or link, between two sectors which are currently discrete, but which are educating what is coming to be regarded as a new social category: that of young people (14-18) of lower academic standing and employability — the so-called 'risk group'. Given these considerations, two themes are now developed. First, the background to the 1977 Munn Report and the 1983 Action Plan is discussed; second, in order to focus on the emerging articulation between non-advanced further education and 'foundation' secondary education, the two courses cited earlier (Social and Vocational Skills and Personal and Social Development) will be compared.

The Munn Report and the Action Plan
In 1977, a national core curriculum for the third and fourth years of Scottish secondary education was recommended (SED, 1977). Its basis was Hirst's 'forms of knowledge', renamed as 'modes of activity'. Although the Munn Report endorsed the subject disciplines, it also allowed for multi-disciplinary courses, one of which was *Contemporary Social Studies (CSS)*. Later, a further multi-disciplinary course, *Social and Vocational Skills (SVS)*, was introduced with a distinctly vocationalist flavour to it, unlike the Hirstian tenor of the Munn Report. Discussion of the details of SVS will be deferred; suffice it to state here that it was introduced with some urgency by the SED, the reason being:

> This new course assumed a considerable importance for the SED who wished to see a credible course emerge as quickly as possible, restoring some of the education service's reputation in the vocationalist field. (Currie and Weir, 1985, page(i))

This emphasis on the vocational suggests that social skills were to be subsumed under vocational skills. Relevant, too, is the fact that the stated rationale of SVS had been lifted word for word from the Further Education Unit (FEU)'s publication *Developing Social and Life Skills: strategies for tutors* (SEB, 1984, page 4). In other words — and this lends weight to the 'articulation' thesis stated earlier — the Scottish Examination Board's SVS guidelines for *secondary* education had drawn heavily upon the FEU's publication relating to *further* education.

Moving from the Munn Report on secondary education, we turn now to the SED's report which calls for a rationalisation of further education: *16-18s in Scotland: An Action Plan* (SED, 1983). Some idea of the background influences to the report can be gleaned from the SED's guide for employers on the Action Plan (SED, 1986). In response to the question: 'Why the need for change?', the guide responds:

(1) encourage more 16-18-year-olds to take up non-compulsory education;
(2) make educational provision more responsive to the needs of employers and students;
(3) take account of the growth of new technology and the changing business scene;
(4) make more efficient use of costly educational facilities;
(5) integrate education and training into a more structured framework to prepare young people for their first job and help them form the *flexible attitudes necessary to deal with life in an increasingly complex society*. (SED, 1986, page 3; emphasis added.)

Earlier, in 1979, the SED had produced a consultative paper raising these matters for public comment (SED, 1979). Some 74 replies were forthcoming from 'educational, commercial, industrial and training interests', thereby revealing 'a general desire for reform' (SED, 1986, page 3). According to Smith, who analysed the replies, no response could be identified from employers' organisations or from the CBI, and only one potential employer responded (Smith, 1985, page 50). Given industry's lack of response to the consultative paper, the justification for the Action Plan could not, therefore, have turned on industry's needs alone. Two other reasons are implied. First, it may well have had more to do with the tidy-mindedness of an officialdom which may have regarded existing provision as too messy: 'To make sense of the curriculum jungle which existed at that time' (Ritchie, quoted in Smith, 1985, page 53). Second, it may have been a ploy to keep at bay the fast-encroaching Manpower Services Commission (MSC): 'There was just no time, particularly with the pace MSC was setting' (Ritchie, quoted in Smith, 1985, page 58). Although the justification for the Action Plan has ostensibly been attributed to one aspect of the 'bureaucratic cognitive style', namely the need to rationalise, nevertheless there is much in it which alludes to pedagogy:

> It follows that within the learning experience a deliberate effort must be made to foster *self-confidence* and *self-reliance*, to encourage *autonomy*, to exercise *independent responsibility*, and to ensure that young people understand how to gain access to advice or information which they require. (SED, 1983, pages 7-8; emphasis added)

Here the accord with the pedagogy of Standard Grade SVS becomes clear: it is a learner-centred one, attempting to further the new flexibility and self-sufficiency required of a service sector economy in which full-time, permanent employment cannot be assured. (It is worth noting that the number of service jobs being created does not exceed the number of manufacturing jobs being lost, especially in the inner-city areas (MSC, 1986).) As with SVS, the Action Plan was written with some urgency: the writing began in the summer of 1982. By November it had been completed. The Minister duly accepted it, thereby ensuring publication in January 1983.

To summarise: the implementation of SVS and the Action Plan represent an emerging correspondence, or 'articulation', between school and college for the less academic young person between 14 and 18. Whilst no formal 'bridge' across the two sectors had been planned in 1983, nevertheless the possibility might have been considered:

> Consideration had been given to attending to '14-18' as a *single entity* but this was rejected, the feeling being that it 'would have been too much for the system to review 14-18 all at once'. (Smith, 1985, page 46, quoting Ritchie; emphasis added)

In what follows, I shall discuss what is considered here to be the vanguard of a new institutional arrangement for the 'less able' 14-18 year-old.

Social and Vocational Skills and Personal and Social Development

Social and Vocational Skills

As stated, two considerations mark SVS: first, it was an urgently implemented addition to Standard Grade, albeit at 'foundation' level (ie the level for the lowest level of achievement — 'general' and 'credit' comprise the middle and highest levels respectively); and second, its multi-disciplinary and pupil-centred focus was a departure from a didactic, subject-centred heritage. More importantly, having been inspired by the English FEU's recommendations in respect of *further* education, SVS applied them in Scotland to *secondary* education, keeping in mind the wider economic context:

> These are years of intensive social and personal development, during which young people have to take very important decisions about their future. What is more, that future holds a great deal of uncertainty and presents many problems. Pupils and schools are faced with a challenge of continuing high levels of unemployment, rapid technological and cultural change and increasing pressures on democratic values. (SED, 1985, page 2)

Social and Vocational Skills requires only an adjustment on the part of the young person to the foreseeable future. It requires a form of self-sufficiency of the type advocated in the last century (Smiles, 1897), thereby allowing the young unemployed worker to cope with the adversity he or she faces. (The scale of this adversity for young school-leavers is considerable: a questionnaire sent in March 1985 to 16 year-old leavers who had left in session 1983-84 produced the following responses in respect of post-school destinations: only 38.4 per cent of males and 44.0 per cent of females were in full-time jobs; the corresponding percentages in YTS were 45.6 and 39.9; and 15.9 and 16.2 per cent respectively were unemployed (Raffe, 1986).) Social and Vocational Skills will engender self-awareness, self-respect, self-assessment and self-evaluation. This celebration of the self requires the individual to take an introspective view of his or her dilemmas. It is reinforced by a pedagogy 'in which the pupils can take increasing responsibility for their own learning and their own actions' (SEB, 1984, page 21). Furthermore, we have the rather ironical situation whereby officialdom (here personified by the convener of the SEB's SVS panel) is inflexibly telling teachers to be flexible:

> However, teachers of S & VS must not only submit details of the experiences and learning outcomes associated with them for moderation (and their sequencing over the two-year period), but they *must* also declare the learning and teaching approaches to be used. And furthermore, the majority of these approaches *must* be pupil-centred. (Carson, 1986, page 49; emphasis added)

The shift towards a service-emphasis in the economy, together with declining opportunities for full-time, permanent employment, requires of the young person a psychological adaptation to it. At present, it is the less academically inclined young person who is most likely to face the personal consequences of this shift. In Scotland, it has been argued that SVS may serve to render the individual passive in the face of this adversity (Hartley, 1986; 1987). But this adaptation will not be achieved easily. It will require a deep and prolonged socialisation period: a mere two-year exposure to SVS would be insufficient. Beyond SVS lies the 16+ course in Personal and Social Development (PSD), to which we now turn.

Personal and Social Development
PSD and SVS seem at first to have different concerns: the latter has more of a vocationalist ring to it. Indeed, of the twenty-one PSD modules, only four course titles imply a clear link with employment. But a careful reading of the PSD guidelines suggests otherwise: that is, PSD is, first, for *all* students:

> If only some students are offered PSD modules and they are seen by staff, students and employees as modules for 'underachievers', then many of the potential benefits are unlikely to be realised. (SED, 1985, page 6)

Moreover, PSD is important for 'vocational competence' (SED, 1985, page 6). Specifically, PSD seeks to further the notion of personal effectiveness by emphasising self-confidence, independence, communication and indeed the whole repertoire of social skills which the young person of (one surmises) a working-class background lacks. One education authority, Lothian, has already recognised the 'content overlap' between SVS and PSD:

> Students moving from satisfactory completion of an SVS course in S4 into a situation where PSD modules are on offer may have difficulty in deciding which will be the best choice of modules given their previous experience in SVS. How will they know whether the module will enable them to extend their abilities or whether it will be a more detailed re-run of their past experience? (MacDonald and Coull, 1986, para 1)

Aside from this perceived bureaucratic messiness over 'content', it is recognised that:

> There will remain, however, a *process similarity* between SVS and PSD where, in both cases there is an emphasis on *Social and Communication Skills, Problem Solving and Decision Making Skills.* (MacDonald and Coull, 1986, para 1; emphasis in original).

Here, then, is the compensatory education of the 1980s trying to re-teach the hidden curriculum to those deemed to be culturally deficient and personally ineffective. Given this commonality of form and content in SVS and PSD, can it be argued that these courses constitute the curricular catalyst for a common educational structure for the lower-achieving 14-18 year-old in Scotland?

SVS and PSD: harbingers of a new institutional structure
Apart from the correspondences between SVS and PSD which have just been defined, what further evidence is there for a new institutional arrangement for low-achieving 14-18 year-olds in Scotland? In England, the beginnings of such an arrangement are already in place. In the

Supporting TVEI document (FEU, 1985), FEU's chief officer notes that the School Curriculum Development Committee/FEU Working Group 'recognises the potential TVEI offers for innovation in the 14-18 curriculum, based on *collaboration between all the relevant partners, principally FE colleges and schools'* (FEU, 1985, page (ii); emphasis added). This has gained greater currency with the publication of the White Paper *Working Together — Education and Training* (DES, 1986). There already exists in England the institution of the tertiary college, albeit for 16-18 year-olds, not 14-18 year-olds. It is not known if, in Scotland, similar plans are afoot, but it would not stretch the imagination too much given the overlap between MSC (Scotland) and the CCC/SED. There are, indeed, a few indications. Take, for example, the CCC's recent call for a modular curriculum structure for the 10-14 age-range:

> 8.132 We recognise that the feasibility of a move towards a modular structure is dependent, not only on educational considerations and teachers' attitudes to them, but also on administrative, and especially timetabling possibilities. These are *dependent on structures and patterns of timetabling and staff developments elsewhere in the school. And, of course, there are reasons to believe that, arising principally from developments in education at 16+, a predominantly modular structure may become the norm in secondary schools.* (CCC, 1986b, page 111; emphasis added)

The significance of this reference to the 'modularisation' of the post-10 curriculum is considerable. Quite apart from epistemological concerns which it provokes (Jonathan, 1987), it would threaten the identity of the subject-centred teacher. Any potential diminution of his or her status would be resisted, particularly by teachers of the more able pupils. On the other hand, the teachers of the multidisciplinary courses, such as SVS, may have a weaker case for resisting modularisation. Thus the modularisation of the secondary school Standard Grade curriculum would probably 'trickle down', for political reasons, from non-advanced 16+ programmes to the 'foundation' level of the Standard Grade where multidisciplinary courses have already been implemented.

If we add to this the SED's active consideration of an expanded role for the Scottish Vocational Education Council (SCOTVEC) whereby 16+ National Certificate modules could be offered to schools at *pre-16 level* (Munro, 1987), then we begin to see the scale of the 'articulation' which is being sought. Doubtless, the SED would couch the move in terms of the usual democratic notion of widening educational opportunity by catering more for the individual needs of young people, but that would also portend a take-over bid for Standard Grade, particularly 'foundation' courses, thereby reducing the remit of the SEB and expanding that of SCOTVEC. Some evidence for this already exists. Currently, PSD modules are being taken in school by *pre*-16 year-olds whose normal Standard Grade equivalent would be the non-modular SVS course at Foundation level. (In 1985-86, those aged under 16 represented 10 per cent of students taking National Certificate modules (SED, 1988, page 2). Before July 1987 this had been more practice than policy, but from August 1987 SCOTVEC's modular foot was wedged firmly in the SEB's door when the SED finally gave approval for the use of National Certificate 16+ modules to 'supplement' S3 and S4 Standard Grade courses (Munro, 1987), and the Consultative Committee on the Curriculum immediately advised education authorities of the interim measures to effect this, pending more 'detailed guidance' (*TES*, 1987, page 6). Already, the politicking has begun. Rand and Young (1988), writing in the journal *16+ Broadcast*, the newsletter of the Curriculum Advice and Support Team (CAST) for 16+, pose the questions:

> Do we need one Scottish examination board only?
> Is it desirable to have two certification systems at 14-18 in Scotland?
> How is *the conflict* [my emphasis] between modules in S3/S4 and Standard Grades to be resolved? (Rand *and* Young, 1988, page 9)

These questions are not those of the authors, but constitute 'issues' generated by the National Course: *The Impact of TVEI on the 14-18 Curriculum and the Professional Development of Teachers*, held (appropriately) on 14-18 September 1987. Furthermore, a three-tier PSD programme is actively under consideration by SCOTVEC. It would comprise school-based PSD modules for pre-16 year-olds, college-based non-advanced PSD modules, and college-based advanced PSD modules. These three levels would be articulated. Such plans would be tantamount to PSD being used as SCOTVEC's Trojan horse to infiltrate Foundation level Standard Grade and sow the seeds of modularisation. In speculating here that there may be an incorporation of 'foundation' level with 16+, rather than of 'credit' and 'general', the reasoning is that such a move would neatly accord with a national TVEI provision which, despite rhetoric that it applies to *all* ability levels, has catered mainly for the *less able* in its first two years (Tenne, 1986). In this way, TVEI, Standard Grade 'foundation' courses and non-advanced 16+ modules could all be integrated to meet the imputed needs of the 'less able'. Spencer's *Modules for All?*, a discussion document referring only to 16+, may have more predictive power than he intended (Spencer, 1984).

To summarise: the speculation here is that we are seeing the beginnings of an articulation of both the form (pupil-centred pedagogy and modularised curricular structure) and the substance (work-based vocational skills and home-based coping skills) of the education for low-achievers in

Scotland. Why have these developments occurred only for this category of young people, and with such urgency? I shall now argue that what is *pedagogically* radical about SVS and PSD may be regarded as *politically* conservative, but not wholly so.

The cult of efficiency and the curbing of criticism

In industrial democracies, two system-maintaining needs must be met: first, efficiency and profitability, or *accumulation;* and second, a set of institutional structures which will render palatable some of industrialism's doubtful consequences, such as high youth unemployment — the need for *legitimation* (O'Connor, 1973). How may we relate these two system needs to PSD and SVS? Take *accumulation.* PSD and SVS will provide the skills necessary for the fast-expanding service industries, thereby contributing to the maximising of profitability. But more than this, their learner-centred pedagogy, with its focus on flexibility and self-control, may provide a worker who has been well socialised into a human relations managerial regime. Consider *legitimation.* Curriculum guideline authors have been quick to stress that SVS and PSD are not simply vocational courses: that is, they contain 'non-work' elements which are meant to benefit the individual, not the economy. This view is questionable. These courses *are* more functional for the economy because they produce an *adaptation* to it on the part of both the young employed *and* unemployed. If the 'social skills' and 'personal and social development' are intended only to produce a psychological adaptation to marginal employment, not to explain it (as seems to be the case), then the *educational* basis of SVS and PSD is weak (Hartley, 1986). In other words, although SVS and PSD offer a radical (i.e. learner-centred) pedagogy, the effect may be politically conservative, because the content which this radical pedagogy transmits will offer little structural analysis of individual adversities. Radical pedagogy will be kept separate from radical curriculum. What may occur is that young people, having been taught to negotiate and to question at college, may feel inclined to do so at work, even where the work regime retains a bureaucratic ethos based on deference rather than debate.

Finally, consider an historical allusion to the speculation being argued here. In an industrial democracy, major structural changes in education often occur in response to upheavals in the economic order. These changes in education, however, are sometimes justified on the basis that they meet the needs of the individual, not those of the economy. This is because, in a democracy, calls for educational change may be heeded more readily if they are thought of as meeting the needs of the individual, not those who control the economy. To illustrate this, take an American precedent. In 1905, the National Association of Manufacturers defined three types of mind: the abstract thinkers; the 'hand-minded' and the generalist. It was no coincidence that these types of mind accorded with the three types of worker needed by businessmen. The IQ testing movement provided the necessary scientific gloss and evidence to prove the existence of these three types of mind (Nasaw, 1979). Having 'proved' that three categories of mind existed, it was but a short step to provide specific educational arrangements which met the intellectual 'needs' of these individuals, in the form of 'tracks' or 'streams'. By so doing, the ideals of democracy and capitalism were reconciled: that is, by 'meeting individual needs' and 'extending opportunity' in a presumed meritocratic order, the appeal to democracy is made; and, by curricular differentiation on behalf of industrialists, the needs of business are also met. Now, however, this threefold classification of mental types is so embedded in educational discourse (hence 'foundation', 'general' and 'credit') that few pause to ponder its historical and political origins. Today, by the SED's own admission, the economy does not require anything like full rates of youth employment. What is now required of education is that it produces many young people who *could be employed*, and who will wait, ready and willing, in the wings of the wage economy. Since the 'needs' of these young people will be different from those of their more 'personally effective' counterparts, surely — so the rhetoric might run — their 'needs' will best be served by a special institutional provision. The price to be paid for this bureaucratic elegance would be to undermine further the comprehensive ideal. If the speculations here were to be realised, then our education service would render a disservice of considerable magnitude to these 'young people'. It would be this: in our society, self-esteem turns on the power, money and status which accrue from our occupation — it does not turn on mere coping with the *lack of* an occupation. To state blandly that, for some, the work ethic may no longer be appropriate, and to state further that it is in *their interest* to prepare 'for leisure', not for work, would be to perpetrate a deception. For the moment, however, education could claim to 'help them to cope', but why do 'they' need help in the first place? Is the fast-expanding catalogue of coping skills no more than a menu from which they can 'choose' in order to contain rather than further their 'personal and social development'? And is the education 'service' expected yet again to provide the solution to economic and social problems which are not of its making?

References
BERGER, P., BERGER, B. *and* KELLNER, H. (1973) *The Homeless Mind.* Harmondsworth: Penguin.

BIDWELL, C. E. (1965) The school as a formal organisation. In: MARCH. J. G. (ed), *A Handbook of Organisations*. New York: Rand McNally.

CARSON, D. (1986) To do with life, *Times Educational Supplement (Scotland)*, 711, 49, June 20 1986.

CONSULTATIVE COMMITTEE ON THE CURRICULUM (1986a) *More Than Feelings of Concern*. Dundee College of Education: CCC and Edinburgh: SED.

CONSULTATIVE COMMITTEE ON THE CURRICULUM (1986b) *Education 10-14 in Scotland*. Dundee College of Education: CCC.

CURRIE, B. *and* WEIR, D. (1985) *The Responsibility of the Teacher: social and vocational skills at foundation and general levels*. Vocational Initiatives Unit: University of Glasgow.

DEPARTMENT OF EDUCATION AND SCIENCE (1986) *Working Together — Education and Training*. Cmnd 9823. London: HMSO.

FURTHER EDUCATION UNIT (1980) *Developing Social and Life Skills: strategies for tutors*. London: FEU and Department of Education and Science.

FURTHER EDUCATION UNIT (1985) *Supporting TVEI*. London: FEU.

HARTLEY, D. (1985) Social education in Scotland: some sociological considerations, *Scottish Educational Review*, 17, 2, 92-98.

HARTLEY, D. (1986) Structural isomorphism and the management of consent in education, *Journal of Education Policy*, 1, 3, 229-237.

HARTLEY, D. (1987) The convergence of learner-centred pedagogy in primary and further education in Scotland: 1965-1985, *British Journal of Educational Studies*, 35, 2, 115-128.

JONATHAN, R. (1987) The case for and against modularisation, *Scottish Educational Review*, 19, 86-98.

MACDONALD, S. *and* COULL, S. (1986) *Articulation from Social and Vocational Skills into the 16+ PSD Modules*. Lothian Regional Council.

MARSDEN, D., TRINDER, C. *and* WAGNER, K. (1986) Measures to reduce unemployment in Britain, France and West Germany. *National Institute Economic Review*, 117, 43-51, August 1986.

MANPOWER SERVICES COMMISSION (1986) Transition from school to work — choices at 16, *Labour Market Quarterly*, pp 13-15, June 1986.

MUNRO, N. (1987) SED opens up schools to SCOTVEC modules, *Times Educational Supplement (Scotland)*, 1079, 1, July 10 1987.

NASAW, D. (1979), *Schooled to Order*. New York: Oxford University Press.

O'CONNOR, J. (1973) *The Fiscal Crisis of the State*. New York: St Martin's Press.

O'NEILL, J. (1986) The disciplinary society: from Weber to Foucault, *British Journal of Sociology*, XXXVII, 1, 42-60.

PLUNKETT, D. (1982) The risk group: education and training policies for disadvantaged young, *Comparative Education*, 18, 1, 39-46.

POLLARD, S. (1965) *The Genesis of Modern Management*. London: Arnold.

RAFFE, D. (1986) Unemployment among 16 and 17 year-old school-leavers, *Employment Gazette*, 94, 6, 274-80, July 1986.

RAND, J. *and* YOUNG, J. (1988) National course report: the impact of TVEI on the 14-18 curriculum and the professional development of teachers, *16+ Broadcast*, 8, 8-11.

SCOTTISH EDUCATION DEPARTMENT (1947) *Secondary Education.* Edinburgh: HMSO.

SCOTTISH EDUCATION DEPARTMENT (1965) *Primary Education in Scotland.* Edinburgh: SED.

SCOTTISH EDUCATION DEPARTMENT (1977) *The Structure of the Curriculum in the Third and Fourth Years of the Scottish Secondary School* The Munn Report). Edinburgh: HMSO.

SCOTTISH EDUCATION DEPARTMENT (1979) *16-18s in Scotland: the first two years of post-compulsory education — a consultative paper.* Edinburgh: SED.

SCOTTISH EDUCATION DEPARTMENT (1983) *16-18s in Scotland: an action plan.* Edinburgh: SED.

SCOTTISH EDUCATION DEPARTMENT (1985) *Guidelines in Personal and Social Development.* Edinburgh: SED.

SCOTTISH EDUCATION DEPARTMENT (1986) *16+ in Scotland — The National Certificate: guide to employers.* Edinburgh: SED.

SCOTTISH EDUCATION DEPARTMENT (1988) The National Certificate 1985-86, *Statistical Bulletin*, 2, F5, 1988.

SCOTTISH EXAMINATION BOARD (1984) *Standard Grade Arrangements in Social and Vocational Skills at Foundation and General Levels in and after 1986.* Dalkeith: SEB.

SMILES, S. (1987) *Self-Help.* London: John Murray.

SMITH, G. (1985) *The Political Context of Educational Change: 16-18s in Scotland Action Plan.* Master's thesis. University of Dundee.

SPENCER, E. (1984) *Modules for All?* Edinburgh: Scottish Council for Research in Education.

STONIER, T. (1979) Changes in Western Society: educational implications. In: SCHULLER, T. *and* MEGARRY, J. (eds) *The World Yearbook of Education: recurrent education and lifelong learning.* London: Kogan Page.

TENNE, R. (1986) TVEI students and subjects studied: the first two years, *Employment Gazette*, 94, 7, 306-310, August 1986.

TIMES EDUCATIONAL SUPPLEMENT (SCOTLAND) CCC outlines policy on use of modules, *Times Educational Supplement (Scotland)*, 1080, 6, July 17 1987.

VALLANCE, E. (1973) Hiding the hidden curriculum, *Curriculum Inquiry*, 38, 5-21.

WELLINGTON, J. J. (1986) The rise of pre-vocational education and the needs of employers, *The Vocational Aspect of Education*, 38, 99, 17-22.

10

Going with the Grain: Youth Training in Transition

David Raffe

Working on a survey series that is regularly extended encourages a conception of social research as soap opera. This chapter presents a further episode in the story of the Youth Training Scheme (YTS). It reviews themes developed in earlier episodes, which covered the first two years of YTS, and continues the story for a further two years, albeit with an exploratory and tentative script.

The main characters
YTS was introduced in 1983 as a one-year scheme of integrated work experience and training for 16 and 17 year-old school leavers. It replaced the Youth Opportunities Programme (YOP) which had been introduced in 1978 to co-ordinate the government's response to youth unemployment (MSC, 1977). Both schemes were run by the Manpower Services Commission, now the Training Commission. YOP had been a temporary measure, available only to unemployed 16-18 year-olds; the average scheme lasted six months and offered work experience, often with an employer; only a minority of schemes provided off-the-job education or training (Greaves *et al,* 1982). By contrast YTS was planned as a permanent scheme, available to all 16 year-old school leavers and to unemployed 17 year-olds. It lasted a full year, of which at least 13 weeks were to be spent off the job. Far from being a last-resort alternative to unemployment, YTS was intended to be 'so attractive to employers and to young people that a minority of young people enter jobs outside the scheme or remain unemployed rather than join the scheme' (MSC, 1982, para 4.8).

In 1986 YTS was relaunched as a two-year scheme (YTS-2); eligibility was extended to all 16 and 17 year-old school leavers; the minimum period off the job was increased to 20 weeks; there was to be more emphasis on occupational competencies, as part of a general drive to establish and promote industry-defined standards; and all trainees were to be offered a chance to pursue recognised vocational qualifications (MSC, 1985, 1986). At the same time YTS-2, like the one-year YTS-1, continued YOP's function of providing a safety net for the young unemployed, with guaranteed places for those who could not find jobs.

This chapter is not only about the transition from school to the labour market; it is also about the transition from YOP to YTS and, more tenta-tively, from YTS-1 to YTS-2. The other characters in our soap opera — our cast of many thousands — are the respondents to the Scottish Young People's Survey. One arm of the SYPS, a cross-sectional postal survey of a sample of the previous session's school leavers, has been conducted bienni-ally since 1977. It provides a series of baselines against which the impact of changing policies and circumstances can be measured. Very often it points to essential continuities beneath the glitter and rhetoric of change.

The story so far
Ideally, the campaign to reform the quantity and quality of youth training in Britain would have started from somewhere else. But this was not to be. For a variety of political, financial and opportunist reasons the new YTS was fostered on the most unlikely of parents, the low-status, unemployment-based YOP (Raffe, 1984). In varying degrees YTS inherited YOP's image, its function as a safety net for the unemployed, and its niche in the labour market.

Analysis of the first Scottish intake to YTS in 1983/4 suggested that the scheme largely continued the unemployment-based functions of its predecessor YOP (Raffe, 1987a). This was reflected in young people's attitudes to YTS, in the qualification levels of entrants to the scheme, in their stated reasons for joining and in their readiness to leave if they found ordinary jobs. There was more evidence of change with respect to boys than girls, but the difference was only one of degree. YTS, it appeared, was the victim of a vicious circle of low status, sustained by the mutual expectations of young people and employers.

A later study reached similar conclusions on the basis of the second intake to YTS (Raffe, 1987b). Drawing attention to the differentiation within YTS, it analysed the constraints on its development and suggested that there were two strategies by which YTS, or particular schemes within it, might hope to break the vicious circle of low status. The first was to provide specific skills in demand in the local labour market and to certify these in a way that retained the confidence of potential employers; the second was to give its trainees favoured access to the information networks through which employers recruited, especially (but not only) through employers using YTS to screen and train their future employees. The analysis suggested that the scope for the first strategy was limited by labour-market conditions, and that the best hope for YTS to enhance its status lay with the second.

The difference between the two strategies roughly corresponds to the difference between training for the external labour market (giving young people skills which they can sell to other employers) and training for the internal labour market (training for an employer's own future needs, including the use of trainees as a flexible recruitment pool). The difference also corresponds to the distinction between an emphasis on the *content* of training and an emphasis on its *context* (*ibid*).

This chapter examines more recent changes in the status of YTS, and asks which of the two strategies it has followed. It extends the earlier studies with data on the fourth intake to YTS and with follow-up data on earlier entrants.

The scale of YTS
Table 1 sets the scene by showing participation on YOP or YTS among school leavers from five alternate sessions. Each column is based on a school leavers' survey and shows the percentage of the previous session's

TABLE 1:   Percentage of school leavers ever on YOP/YTS

	YOP			YTS-1	YTS-2
	1979	1981	1983	1985	1987
School leavers:					
All	17	29	40	40	44
males	19	31	41	43	48
females	16	28	38	37	41
Early leavers	24	41	57	59	65
males	26	42	58	61	68
females	21	40	57	57	61
Later leavers	5	11	19	17	18
males	4	10	19	17	18
females	6	11	19	17	19
Labour-market entrants:					
All	21	38	54	54	59
males	22	38	53	55	61
females	20	38	55	52	58
Early leavers	25	44	62	63	70
males	26	42	59	63	70
females	23	45	66	63	69
Later leavers	8	20	36	33	36
males	6	21	36	33	33
females	10	20	36	32	37

leavers who had at least started a YOP or YTS scheme by the survey date in the following spring. Leavers surveyed in 1979, 1981 and 1983 were covered by YOP; those surveyed in 1985 by the one-year YTS and in 1987 (mostly) by the two-year YTS. Participation on schemes rose from 17 per cent of 1977/8 leavers (surveyed in 1979) to 44 per cent of 1985/6 leavers (surveyed in 1987). However, most of this increase occurred under YOP and reflected the rapid rise in youth unemployment in the early 1980s. Participation levelled off after YTS-1 replaced YOP but then increased slightly under YTS-2.

By 1987, YTS-2 recruited nearly two-thirds (65 per cent) of early leavers (defined here to include all who left by Christmas of fifth year). It recruited 59 per cent of all leavers entering the labour market, and 70 per cent of early leavers entering the labour market. It recruited more boys than girls, but this was mainly because more boys left school early and more entered the labour market. Participation has also varied regionally, partly reflecting different labour market conditions (Tomes, 1987).

The image of YTS
Young people's attitudes to YTS have been predominantly instrumental. Their views on the scheme, and their propensity to enter it, have reflected their perceptions of the short-term and long-term pay-offs from participation. Since YTS schemes have varied widely in organisation, content and prospects, it is not surprising that young people's attitudes to YTS have also varied. Nevertheless, we can discern patterns beneath the variation. Young people in successive surveys tended to be more positive about particular schemes than about YTS in general. Moreover, when asked about YTS in general, sample members expressed more favourable attitudes about the ways it could benefit individuals than about the motives behind the scheme, whether of government or employers. This cynicism partly reflected a pervasive 'folk mythology' of YTS and its purposes, but it also reflected young people's perceptions of (and resentment of) the YTS allowance, the treatment of trainees and their job prospects. It may be aggravated by the withdrawal of benefit from non-participants in 1988: many young people appeared to reject both the normative and the empirical assumptions underlying the argument that they should invest in their occupational futures through YTS (Raffe *and* Smith, 1987). At the same time, this poor image of YTS, and widespread cynicism about its motives, was also a legacy of YOP and of the unemployment-based functions inherited from YOP (Raffe, 1987a).

Comparisons between 1985 sample members (covered by YTS-1) and 1987 sample members (mostly covered by YTS-2) showed only a small 'improvement' in general attitudes towards the scheme (Raffe, 1989, forthcoming). On this evidence, the launch of YTS-2 in 1986, and the associated publicity campaign, had only a modest impact. (Those who recall this campaign, memorable for Spikey Dodds and Tracey Logan, may not be surprised.) More encouraging for YTS were the findings that YTS trainees had more favourable attitudes than other young people, that trainees' attitudes 'improved' substantially after joining the scheme, and that the attitudes of YTS-2 trainees were significantly more positive than those of trainees on YTS-1. But the cynicism persisted. A majority even of YTS-2 trainees in 1987 saw YTS as a 'source of cheap labour' and as 'just to keep unemployment figures down'.

The educational status of YTS trainees

For YTS to improve on YOP's status as an unemployment-based scheme, it needed to attract young school leavers to it in preference to 'ordinary' jobs. Otherwise, its scale and composition would be a mere reflection of youth unemployment: and with the projected tightening of the youth labour market (NEDO, 1988) it would wither away, to survive at best as a rump of schemes for the most disadvantaged workers or in unemployment blackspots.

A good measure of YTS' progress in this respect is the level of school qualifications of its intake, relative to other labour-market entrants. For various reasons, better-qualified school leavers have been much more successful in finding jobs. If YTS increased its recruitment of better-qualified school leavers, especially relative to YOP, this would suggest that more 'employable' school leavers were choosing YTS in preference to ordinary jobs. We use data from the 1981, 1983, 1985 and 1987 surveys to compare patterns of entry to YOP, to YTS-1 and to YTS-2. In each case we compare the school qualifications of YOP/YTS trainees with those of other labour-market entrants who had not gone on YOP/YTS. The analysis is not presented in detail here but its main conclusions are summarised below.

First, YOP recruited disporportionately from the less qualified. This is not surprising; it reflects the fact that the scheme only recruited unemployed young people, who tended to be less qualified.

Second, YTS also recruited disproportionately from the less qualified, but to a lesser extent. Relative to YOP, YTS was more successful in attracting school leavers in the middle ('O' grade) range of educational attainment, but it did not increase recruitment among school leavers with no 'O' grades or with Highers.

Third, this trend continued between 1985 (YTS-1) and 1987 (YTS-2), but the difference between YTS-1 and YTS-2 was much smaller than that between YOP and YTS-1. (However, the survey data may underestimate the increase in 'status' of YTS-2. Increasing numbers of entrants have had employee status: they tend to be well qualified, but may describe themselves in the survey data as in ordinary jobs rather than on YTS.)

Fourth, YTS reduced its recruitment among sixth-year leavers, presumably because many were aged 18 and ineligible for the scheme. This explains the relative decline in entry among Highers-qualified leavers described above.

Fifth, YTS recruited many more early leavers (those leaving by the Christmas of fifth year) than either fifth- or sixth-year leavers, and it is among the early leavers that YTS made most progress in changing the character of its intake. Recruitment to YTS among early leavers was significantly less skewed towards the less qualified than recruitment to YOP had been. We infer that YTS attracted several 'O' grade-qualified minimum-age school leavers in preference to ordinary jobs. However, even among early leavers, the average qualifications of YTS entrants were still, in 1987, lower than those of direct entrants to employment, although there was a substantial overlap between the two groups.

YTS is internally differentiated; its increased ability to attract better qualified school leavers may reflect the status and attraction of particular schemes rather than of YTS as a whole. Subject to this, we conclude that YTS has significantly enhanced its status relative to YOP among early leavers, presumably because several schemes have attracted 'O' grade qualified youngsters to enter them in preference to available ordinary jobs. However, YTS has continued, like YOP, to recruit disporportion-ately from early leavers, and it has virtually stopped recruiting any 18 year-old leavers at all. Since early leavers tend to have fewer qualifications, this sets a limit on the ability of YTS as presently organised to increase its status further, at least as measured by educational indicators. Attainment and status in the British educational system are strongly associated with continuity and survival through its post-compulsory stages. It is unlikely that this association has materially weakened with the introduction of YTS. The implication is that the tight age-linking of YTS guarantees at least a relatively low status for the scheme. It may also mean that the status of YTS is defined increasingly directly in educational terms (via early leaving) rather than through the labour market (via unemployment).

Routes to employment
Given that YTS has increased its status among early leavers, how has it done this? An obvious explanation is that YTS, or at least some schemes, have provided routes to desired employment. To pursue this explanation we turn to the other and newer arm of the Scottish Young Peoples Survey

—the longitudinal survey of school year groups, surveyed over the three years following the end of compulsory schooling. The analyses and data described below are based on the first two sweeps (in 1985 and 1986) of the first year group to be surveyed longitudinally. This comprises young people who had been in fourth year in 1983/4.

Main and Shelly (1988) compared early leavers who had been on (one-year) YTS in October 1984 with those who had been unemployed; allowing for the different characteristics of YTS trainees and the unemployed, they concluded that YTS gave about a 20 percentage point advantage with respect to employment chances 18 months later. However, although this may demonstrate that YTS was preferable to unemployment, it does not necessarily follow that YTS was preferable to direct entry to employment for those who had the choice. For this, some comparisons between those who entered employment via YTS and those who entered directly may be appropriate. Main and Shelly found that the range of jobs held by former YTS trainees in 1986 was broadly similar to the range of jobs held by direct entrants to employment. Former trainees were slightly more likely to find jobs in construction, and slightly less likely to work in manufacturing, but there was no evidence of their being 'locked into' particular occupations or industries. They tended to earn lower wages, but this appeared to be a consequence of the greater training still being received by former YTS trainees at the time of the comparison. (Young people receiving training are assumed to have lower current productivity and therefore lower wages.)

In interpreting the conclusions of such research, we must bear in mind the enormous diversity of YTS. Clearly some schemes were much more likely than others to provide routes to desired employment and therefore to attract young school leavers in preference to jobs outside YTS. Unfortunately, many of the factors which may differentiate YTS schemes are difficult to measure in large-scale surveys where young people, rather than scheme providers, are the main source of data.

Future work on the surveys will continue to study young people's routes through YTS, and to compare them with other routes into the labour market. This work will take advantage of a further sweep of the year group described above in autumn 1987, more than three years after the end of compulsory schooling for most sample members, and of data on new year groups first contacted in 1987 and 1989.

Internal and external labour markets
Although much work remains to be done on the routes to employent opened up by YTS, we can begin to comment on the strategy it has followed to raise its status.

Table 2 covers members of the year group who were on one-year YTS in spring 1985. It summarises their experiences of (un)employment after leaving the scheme. A third found jobs in the internal labour market, with their YTS employers or sponsors. Another third found full-time jobs in the external labour market, that is with other employers, and most of the remaining third were unemployed up to spring 1986.

TABLE 2:   **Destinations after YTS: percentages of young people on YTS in spring 1985 who had left it by spring 1986**

	All	Males	Females
Full-time job with YTS employer or sponsor:			
before completing scheme	7	3	11
on completing scheme	27	30	22
Full-time job elsewhere:			
before completing scheme	11	10	13
on completing scheme	8	8	7
later, after period of unemployment	13	14	12
Unemployed on leaving YTS and in spring 1986	30	32	27
Others	4	2	7
Total (n=932)	100	99	99

The table shows a clear difference between trainees who found jobs in the internal and in the external labour markets respectively. Most of the internal recruits moved straight into jobs at the end of their schemes. Most of the external recruits either left YTS early, presumably to take up jobs while they were available, or experienced a spell of unemployment between YTS and employment. Other data (not shown in the table) suggest that the internal recruits enjoyed more stable employment: they were more likely to be still in full-time employment in spring 1986. They were also more likely to be getting further training in their current jobs.

Table 3 makes further comparisons between internal and external recruits. It presents three measures of the 'relevance' of their YTS training to the current jobs of those in full-time employment in spring 1986. The internal recruits tended to be working in the same occupational areas as their YTS schemes, to think that YTS had helped them to get their present jobs (not surprisingly, perhaps) and to think that what they had learnt on YTS had helped them to do their jobs. By contrast, for many trainees who found jobs externally, the connection between YTS and their subsequent employment was doubtful. Only half were employed in the same occupational areas as their YTS schemes. Only four in ten felt that being on YTS had helped them get their present jobs.

TABLE 3: 'Relevance' of YTS to current employment, by whether kept on by YTS employer: young people on YTS in spring 1985 and in full-time employment in spring 1986

	All		Males		Females	
	kept on	not	kept on	not	kept on	not
% in same occupation as YTS	84	49	81	40	88	59
'Do you think that being on a YTS scheme helped you to get your present job?' (% yes)	94	41	91	34	97	49
'Do you think that what you learned on your YTS scheme has helped you to do this job?'						
it has helped a lot	63	23	64	17	61	31
it has helped a little	30	36	29	37	32	34
it has not helped at all	7	41	8	46	7	35

These data allow a crude quantification of the relative importance of the two strategies, discussed earlier, for raising the status of YTS. Of all year group members on YTS in spring 1985 only about one in eight found jobs with other employers with the help (as they described it) of YTS. The proportion doing so and remaining in the same occupational area was about one in ten. Even some of these may have found work because of contacts (access to information networks) gained through YTS, rather than through skills gained on the scheme (Knasel *and* Watts, 1987). By contrast, one in three found jobs with scheme sponsors, in the internal labour market.

YTS appears to have raised its status primarily by providing opportunities for employment with scheme employers. It seems to have conformed to a British pattern of training for the internal labour market and for firms' own needs; particular schemes and occupational areas may be exceptions, but the general marketability of YTS training in the external labour market is yet to be demonstrated. (There is some supporting evidence for this claim from studies of employers (Chapman *and* Tooze, 1985; Roberts *et al*, 1986, 1987) but most studies of employers have focused on their roles as YTS providers and as internal recruiters, rather than external recruiters, of trainees. This bias in the research is itself indirect support for the present argument.)

It is apparent from Tables 2 and 3 that these conclusions apply somewhat less strongly to females than males. This is consistent with long-standing gender differences in training patterns in Britain: girls have been more likely than boys to acquire vocational education or training for use in the external, rather than the internal, labour market.

Vocational education, training and the youth labour market
These data describe one-year YTS. The two-year scheme, with its focus on industry-defined standards and its offer of recognised certification to all trainees, may appeal more successfully to the external market. But its success here may be restricted by its very success in respect of the internal labour market. Trainees who are not kept on by YTS sponsors may find themselves doubly stigmatised, not only as YTS trainees but also as the sponsoring firm's cast-offs (Roberts *et al*, 1987). Young people similarly tend to treat the prospect of retention as a criterion of a good scheme. More generally, the success of YTS in the external labour market may depend less on improvements in the content of YTS than on reforms of its context. In many occupational areas, and below a certain level of skill, British employees seem largely to disregard vocational qualifications as criteria for selection, unless backed up by considerable experience.

The early experience of the 16-plus Action Plan is relevant here. This has replaced virtually all non-advanced vocational education with a system of modules, each of notional 40 hours' duration, assessed by a single National Certificate (SED, 1983). Both the content and the structure of the modular system are highly compatible with YTS; National Certificate modules are the main source of the off-the-job training for YTS in Scotland (and their use to certificate work-based elements is being explored, if cautiously). The modular system has enjoyed success on several fronts; it appears to be popular with many employers and YTS managing agents as a flexible and convenient source of off-the-job provision for their employees, apprentices and trainees. In other words, it appears to have provided effectively for the internal labour market. Its main problems relate to the external market. Analysis of data on the year group described above, casts doubt on the extent to which National Certificate modules have helped young people find jobs

(Raffe, 1988). This analysis is based on the first year group to be affected by the Action Plan, and things may improve when employers become more familiar with the new Certificate. But it suggests that many of the problems experienced by YTS in relation to the external labour market lie outside YTS itself, in the selection criteria currently applied in the British youth labour market.

A similar conclusion can be drawn from the early Scottish experience of the Training Commission's own Technical and Vocational Education Initiative (TVEI) for 14-18 year-olds. Although employers have generally supported its objectives, they have been reluctant to change their selection criteria in favour of young people who have pursued TVEI's more vocationally oriented curriculum, or of older school leavers who have completed a four-year TVEI programme. Together with the conservative criteria of selection to university, this seems to have prevented TVEI from boosting 16 year-old staying-on rates in full-time education; more TVEI students have left school at 16 to join YTS than have remained on TVEI (Bell *et al*, 1988; Bell *and* Howieson, 1988).

The tentative hypothesis of this chapter is that YTS has raised its status, at least within the limits implied by its age-linking, by going with the grain of the British youth labour market. This tends to be characterised by a preference in many occupational areas for recruiting at 16, by a reluctance to give broadly based vocational curricula and qualifications much weight as criteria for selection, and by a tendency to train (if at all) for an employer's own and immediate needs. As noted earlier, these characteristics are more generally true of the male than of the female market; moreover, different considerations apply to the adult market and to jobs requiring higher levels of skill. These characteristics have given rise to a system of vocational education and training that is insufficient in quantity, too specific in content, and front-end loaded in age terms. They account for the failure of British education to develop a substantial full-time technical or vocational sector comparable with many European countries. They account for the failure, in many occupational areas, to develop a work-based system whose products are highly marketable in the external labour market. They may also account for the way that YTS has developed, and its apparent emphasis on training for the internal rather than the external labour market.

One implication of this analysis is that YTS must fight to maintain and enhance the level, breadth and transferability of its training, as these are typically threatened when training is carried out for the internal labour market (Roberts *et al*, 1986, chapters 6 and 7). This may become harder if a tighter youth labour market weakens the Training Commission's bargaining power by making it more dependent on employers to maintain

YTS as their preferred avenue of recruitment and training; and it may not be helped by the current policy of relying on industry to define its own training standards (MSC, 1986).

But could not more be done to increase the value of YTS training (or indeed of TVEI or the National Certificate) in the external labour market? The recent emphasis in the education-industry debate — on getting education to change in line with industry's needs — should now be reversed; in some respects, at least, it is now time for industry to change. If employers are sincere in asking the education and training system to produce a more competent, versatile and better prepared workforce, they must put their money where their mouths are: not only by providing more training themselves, but also by changing their recruitment and selection practices to favour the education and training programmes that attempt to respond to their needs.

Conclusion

Many of the plots of soap operas are almost endlessly recycled. The story of YTS seems to have hit on one of the oldest plots of all: the indifference of many British employers to broadly-based vocational education and training. Perhaps the plot can be given a new twist this time. Or is this unlikely while the same employers are increasingly given responsibility for writing the script?

Acknowledgements

An earlier version of this chapter was presented to the workshop on Research on Employment and Unemployment at Caxton House, London, in January 1988. The workshop was funded by the Department of Employment (DE) and the Economic and Social Research Council (ESRC). The Scottish Young Peoples Survey is conducted by the Centre for Educational Sociology (CES) at the University of Edinburgh in conjunction with the Scottish Education Department (SED). It is funded by the SED, the Industry Department for Scotland, the Manpower Services Commission and the DE; work on this paper was supported by the ESRC (grant no. C00280004), of which the CES is a Designated Research Centre. The views expressed in this paper are the author's, and are not necessarily shared by any of the bodies mentioned above.

References

BELL, C. and HOWIESON, C. (1988) The view from the hutch: educational guinea-pigs speak about TVEI. In: RAFFE, D. (ed) *Education and the Youth Labour Market: schooling and scheming*. Lewes: Falmer.

BELL, C., HOWIESON, C., KING, K. *and* RAFFE, D. (1988) *Liaisons Dangereuses? Education-Industry Relationships in the First Scottish TVEI Pilot Projects: an evaluation report.* University of Edinburgh, Centre for Educational Sociology/Department of Education.

CHAPMAN, P. G. *and* TOOZE, M. J. (1985) *Youth Training in Scotland: a review of progress.* University of Dundee, Department of Economics.

GREAVES, K., GOSTYN, P. *and* BONSALL, C. (1982) *Off the Job Training on YOP.* Research and Development Series, 12. Sheffield: Manpower Services Commission.

KNASEL, E. G. and WATTS, A. G. (1987) Timing of employment selection within the Youth Training Scheme, *British Journal of Education and Work,* 1, 2, 91-102.

MAIN, B. G. M. and SHELLY, M. A. (1988) Does it pay young people to go on YTS? In: RAFFE, D. (ed), *Education and the Youth Labour Market: schooling and scheming.* Lewes: Falmer.

MANPOWER SERVICES COMMISSION (1977) *Young People and Work* (The Holland Report). London: MSC.

MANPOWER SERVICES COMMISSION (1982) *Youth Task Group Report.* Sheffield: MSC.

MANPOWER SERVICES COMMISSION (1985) *Development of the Youth Training Scheme: a report.* Sheffield: MSC.

MANPOWER SERVICES COMMISSION (1986) *Qualifications in YTS: guidance for developing qualifications in YTS.* Sheffield: MSC.

NATIONAL ECONOMIC DEVELOPMENT OFFICE (1988) *Young People and the Labour Market: a challenge for the 1990s.* London: NEDO and Training Commission.

RAFFE, D. (1984) Youth unemployment and the MSC 1977-83. In: McCRONE, D. (ed) *Scottish Government Yearbook 1984.* University of Edinburgh, Unit for the Study of Government in Scotland.

RAFFE, D. (1987a) Small expectations: the first year of the Youth Training Scheme. In: JUNANKAR, P. N. (ed) *From School to Unemployment: the labour market for young people.* Basingstoke: Macmillan.

RAFFE, D. (1987b) The context of the Youth Training Scheme: an analysis of its strategy and development, *British Journal of Education and Work,* 1, 1, 1-31.

RAFFE, D. (1988) Modules and the strategy of institutional versatility: the first two years of the 16 plus Action Plan in Scotland. In: RAFFE, D. (ed) *Education and the Youth Labour Market: schooling and scheming.* Lewes: Falmer.

RAFFE, D. (1989, forthcoming) Longitudinal and historical change in young people's attitudes to the Youth Training Scheme, *British Educational Research Journal,* 15, 2.

RAFFE, D. and SMITH, P. (1987) Young people's attitudes to YTS: the first two years, *British Educational Research Journal,* 13, 3, 241-260.

ROBERTS, K., DENCH, S. and RICHARDSON, D. (1986) *The Changing Structure of Youth Labour Markets.* Research Paper, 59. London; Department of Employment.

ROBERTS, K., DENCH, S., RICHARDSON, D. *and* PHILLIPS, D. (1987) *The Dual YTS.* University of Liverpool, Department of Sociology.

SCOTTISH EDUCATION DEPARTMENT (1983) *16-18s in Scotland: an action plan.* Edinburgh: SED.

TOMES, N. (1987) Regional participation in the Youth Training Scheme, *Scottish Economic Bulletin,* 36, 30-34.

11

The Transition from Beginning Student-Teacher to Fluent Classroom Teacher

Donald McIntyre

What are the processes and patterns of learning which transform beginning student-teachers into fluent classroom teachers in the course of perhaps five or ten years?

Whether we consider this question as of fundamental importance or as of merely 'academic' interest will depend on our view of the relationship between the teaching and the learning of beginning teachers. Since teacher education was institutionalised in the nineteenth century, those of us who are teacher educators have generally seemed very confident in our knowledge of what is involved in being a good teacher, although this confidence has been vested in a bewildering variety of competing orthodoxies, ranging from Herbart to Habermas, from Homer Lane to Hirst. Because of this confidence in our knowledge of what student-teachers should become, our inclination has naturally been to concern ourselves primarily with *what* we teach them, and to a lesser extent with *how* we teach them. Given such a starting-point, questions of what student-teachers and beginning teachers learn, and of how they learn, tend to be reduced to questions about how far they have come to be the way we want them to be.

Such an emphasis cannot be entirely wrong. If we did not have good ideas about what would be valuable knowledge for beginning teachers, then the whole enterprise of initial teacher education would be directionless and therefore of little value; and it is abundantly clear that that is not the case. Nonetheless, our concern with the *teaching* of beginning teachers has, I believe, led us to pay insufficient attention to their *learning*. The distinction becomes important only if it can be shown that what beginning teachers learn, and how they learn, are relatively independent of their tutors' and supervising teachers' plans for their learning; but if that can be shown to be the case, then an understanding of the patterns and processes of beginning teachers' learning would be as important in the planning of teacher education programmes as an understanding of what they ought to learn.

Arguments for attending to beginning teachers' learning
What grounds are there for believing that beginning teachers' learning is substantially influenced by factors other than their teacher education programmes?

First, there is the fact that prospective teachers have highly elaborated ideas about the task of teaching and the work of schoolteachers even before they enter teacher education programmes. Not only is teaching an everyday activity in which people engage in their homes, with their peers, and in most organisations to which they belong, but also people grow up seeing far more of the activities of teachers than they do of any other occupational group. Although there is a lack of evidence about which kinds of biographical events most influence people's ideas about teaching, the 'apprenticeship of observation' (Lortie, 1975) — which, as participant observation, is often highly emotionally charged — is likely to provide a very rich repertoire of images of teaching, and of ideas about the purposes of teaching and about the strategies and tactics which should and should not be adopted. Whatever the source, the complex and firmly established understandings and commitments which people bring with them to teacher education programmes are likely to be only slowly and partially modified by these programmes or even by the experience of school-teaching. Learning will certainly occur as a result of new experiences and ideas, but the nature of that learning will be substantially determined by already established ways of making sense of teaching and schooling.

A second reason why student-teachers' learning may often diverge from what others have planned for them is that they themselves are likely to have definite priorities about what they need to learn. Fuller (1969) has indeed used the idea of *concerns* as the key concept in her theorisation of teacher development, and she and others have demonstrated systematic, if not straightforward, variations among beginning teachers in their concerns. Student-teachers have their own *agendas* of things they need to do and things they need to learn, and the demands of teacher education programmes are not necessarily of dominant importance in shaping these agendas.

For example, for many student-teachers, *being accepted as a teacher* in their placement schools appears to be very high on their agendas. Perhaps they view the process of becoming a teacher not as one of learning, but rather as one of being tried for one's suitability; perhaps it is simply socially uncomfortable to be neither a pupil nor a teacher. Whatever the reasons, where this is a dominant concern college courses may be viewed as irrelevant unless they are seen as helpful for this relatively immediate purpose. In the school, it will be the success of their classroom *performance* which preoccupies student-teachers with this kind of concern, and learning from experience in order to develop one's *competence* as a teacher may seem a very remote and other-worldly concern.

Beginning teachers' concerns and agendas may often be based on very misguided ideas about the nature of teaching, such as that it is possible to have a kind of generalised recipe knowledge which can be applied to particular situations. That such aspirations are misconceived, however, does not reduce their importance in shaping both the process and the content of the learning that occurs.

A third reason for viewing beginning teachers' learning as relatively independent of what is planned in their teacher education programmes is that there is increasing evidence of their capacity to find their own ways of making sense of the realities they experience. In this respect they are not of course different from other people; but whereas they may largely assimilate, as intelligent people, what they are taught as mathematicians, chemists or historians, they may be much more ready to reject uncomfortable information when it relates to themselves as classroom practitioners, and to find less stressful ways of understanding events.

One common phenomenon is student-teachers' attribution of their teaching problems to their status as student-teachers and to a related lack of respect from pupils and a lack of freedom to act as they would wish. Lacey (1977) noted also that student-teachers learned to attribute the blame for their failures either to the weaknesses of 'the system' or to those of their pupils. Weinstein (1988) provides another example, in this case with reference to student-teachers who had not yet begun their student teaching: she demonstrates a strong and pervasive tendency among the student-teachers in one institution to 'unrealistic optimism', a belief that they will experience less than their peers the difficulties that they know to be commonly experienced by beginning teachers. Whatever the source of this unrealistic optimism, its impact on student-teachers' motivation to learn ways of surmounting the difficulties must be considerable.

Once again, a recognition that student teachers are misguided in attributing unusual strengths to themselves or in attributing their present problems to sources beyond themselves should not mislead us from also recognising the significance of these attribution patterns in shaping the learning of beginning teachers.

A fourth reason for viewing beginning teachers' learning as not simply the consequence of planned teacher education is the social complexity of the processes of learning about teaching. Even within the framework of teacher education programmes, the student-teacher encounters a variety of sources of ideas, perhaps most notably in differing messages from college tutors and from school placement staffrooms, but also more generally in the diverse viewpoints expressed by different departments or individuals within colleges and within schools; and in addition there is a diversity of practice to be observed within the different institutions. Furthermore, there are two other very important sources of opinion, the pupils whom student-teachers teach and their student-teacher peers. It is thus not difficult to find either legitimation or challenge of their existing perceptions and practices, whichever they seek.

Lacey (1977) exemplifies these possibilities when he describes 'collectivisation' and 'privatisation' as two major types of strategy through which student-teachers deal with problems of the teaching situation: when appropriate, the problem might be 'shared by the group whose collective opinions legitimise the displacement of blame', while in other circumstances the same student teachers might find it wiser to keep quiet about their problems and their ways of dealing with them.

The social situation of student-teachers is further complicated by the fact that the different socially significant sources of information and opinion are also different audiences. While student-teachers may find help and support from different sources in facing their problems, they also need to persuade their different audiences about the acceptability of their views and practices as teachers. Shipman (1967) suggested that student-teachers find it necessary and possible to offer systematically different impressions of their views and practices to supervising teachers and college tutors. Lacey (1977) again indicates the variety of different strategies which may be successfully employed, ranging from more or less conscious deception and evasion to more sophisticated strategies, such as the following:

> The teacher-tutor was at all times more recognisant of the concrete teaching situation, whereas the E-tutor preferred to talk in theoretical terms. I balanced the two viewpoints by recognising the constraints which governed their thinking. (Lacey, 1977, page 93)

The possibility of drawing on different sources and the need to cater for different audiences necessarily mean that the processes and patterns of beginning teachers' learning are considerably more complex than those generally planned in teacher education programmes. In addition, however, recognition of this social complexity forces one to an appreciation of the difficulty of studying this learning.

One very simple final reason may be given for studying beginning teachers' learning in terms other than those of initial teacher education programmes. Such programmes come to an end at the point when student-teachers are viewed as ready to become employed as teachers. In the United Kingdom at least, they are not generally followed by any substantial planned provision to facilitate the professional learning of beginning teachers during their first years of employment. Yet there can be no doubt that it is during these years that much of the important learning of beginning teachers occurs. At that stage teacher education programmes do not provide a framework for understanding what is being learned and how, simply because any such programmes are at best marginal to the learning opportunities and activities which occur.

Approaches to studying the transition from beginning student-teacher to experienced teacher
Concern with the ways in which beginning teachers change as they go through their initial professional education and their first years of teaching is far from new. It has indeed been the focus of many enquiries over the last three or four decades. Have these studies not led to the kind of understanding which has been argued here to be necessary?

One very widely used approach was in terms of the attitudes or ideologies of beginning teachers, with evidence being gathered in terms of scores on attitude scales at successive stages. Typical among the instruments used were the Manchester Opinion Scales, contrasting naturalism with idealism, radicalism with conservatism, and tender-mindedness with toughmindedness (e.g. Butcher, 1965; Morrison *and* McIntyre, 1967) and the Pupil Control Ideology scale, contrasting custodial and humanistic approaches to classroom control (e.g. Hoy, 1969). More recent studies in this tradition (e.g. McArthur, 1981) have tended to study larger samples of beginning teachers over longer periods of time.

The results of such studies have been fairly consistent: during their years as student-teachers, people generally become more progressive, more radical, more humanistic and more tendtminded in their responses; but in their first years of teaching these changes tend to be reversed. Similar reversals during periods of school placement for student-teachers have also been found. There have, however, been exceptions to these general trends: the broad liberalising tendency does not seem to occur in all colleges, and the reversal tendency does not seem to occur in relatively progressive school environments, such as those widely found in infant schools.

Such conclusions, interesting as they are, must be interpreted with some caution. For example, they take no account of the possibly changing salience of different issues for beginning teachers as they progress through teacher education programmes and into employment as teachers, nor of the possible significance of the immediate social contexts in which responses to the attitude scales are made at different stages.

Another approach, which has addressed directly the question of what is salient to respondents, has been that of studying beginning teachers' *problems* at different stages, as these have been perceived by the beginning teachers themselves. Veenman (1984) reviews 83 such studies conducted in various countries between 1960 and 1983. Again these different studies show substantially consistent results with, for example, classroom discipline, motivating students, and dealing with individual differences recurring persistently as the three most common problems. However, as Veenman himself notes:

> In spite of the general agreement on the kind of problems beginning teachers experience, it appears that these findings are too general in that they do not consider the various teacher characteristics or individual differences which may influence teachers' perceptions and performance. Nor do they identify the context so that we can understand how environments with varying supports and challenges affect the beginning teacher. Recently, several approaches have been developed to look more carefully at the process of becoming a teacher. (Veenman, 1984, page 160)

These three weaknesses identified by Veenman, of lack of attention to individual differences, to contextual influences, and to the processes of change, apply not only to the *perceived problems* type of study but also to the *attitude scales* type.

The earliest influential attempt to confront the third of these problems was Fuller's (1969; Fuller *and* Bown, 1975) theory of teacher development in terms of the changing *concerns* of beginning teachers. From an initial stage of naive self-confident 'no concern', she suggested, student-teachers tended to move to one of self-concern, or concern for survival, during their student teaching and sometimes in their first year of teaching. They then tended to move, after these concerns had been met, to a phase of concern about 'the teaching situation', which might incorporate both concerns to develop their own skills and concerns about limitations imposed by organisational, resource and time constraints. Finally, when all these other concerns had been resolved, the mature teacher's concern would be focused primarily on the learning and the needs of his or her pupils.

While some investigations have produced evidence broadly consistent with Fuller's suggested phases, her formulations, like those in terms of attitudinal dimensions and characteristic problems, take no significant account of differences among individuals or differences among contexts; and that too is apparent from the results of studies informed by this framework. While Fuller's theory has the major merit of being concerned with the processes through which beginning teachers learn, it would have been very surprising if empirical studies had shown that beginning teachers, irrespective of their background, their values, their teacher education programmes and their varied experiences, consistently developed through the suggested phases.

Theories such as Fuller's can certainly offer helpful insights, and the concept of 'concerns' is certainly of value in directing our attention towards the issues to which student-teachers or teachers themselves give priority. If we are to understand the processes whereby they develop, however, this can only be a starting-point: we must also attend to the ways in which they construe the tasks of teaching, the ways they set about these tasks, and the processes through which new perceptions and ideas are acquired which lead these understandings and ways of doing things to develop. Given the complexity of teaching, it is inevitable that the process of learning to teach will be equally complex: it is the complexities of this learning that we need to understand.

Since the mid-seventies there have been various initiatives which have moved in this direction, each seeking a more detailed and subtler understanding of the processes whereby beginning teachers learn and become experienced. Three contrasting but perhaps complementary approaches will be outlined.

Feiman-Nemser and Buchmann (1985, 1987) conducted an intensive study of the progress of six elementary education students through two years of undergraduate teacher education in one or other of two contrasting innovative programmes. Regular interviews with the students were grounded on systematic observation of their courses and of their student teaching and were complemented by frequent informal conversations with the students and with tutors and teachers working with them. On the basis of the extensive evidence gathered in these ways, rich accounts were generated of the personal backgrounds, concerns, aspirations, understandings, problems, experiences and self-assessments of each of the student-teachers, and of how these changed.

It is in their framework for interpreting these very full accounts that the work of Feiman-Nemser and Buchmann is perhaps most distinctive. They adopt an explicit theoretical position about the tasks required of teaching and teacher preparation:

> Teaching, in sum, requires knowledge of subject matter, persons, and pedagogy. It demands principled and strategic thinking about ends, means and their consequences. Most important, it requires interactive skills and serious commitment to foster student learning.
>
> (Feiman-Nemser *and* Buchmann, 1987, pages 256-7)

Given such a framework, the interpretations (and probably to some extent the accounts themselves) inevitably tend to focus on the gaps between what happened and what was ideally desirable; in particular, emphasis is placed on the 'pitfalls of experience'. Problems, and explanations of these problems, are presented largely in terms of external judgmental views of the student-teachers (e.g. 'her basic insecurity', 'a limited view of practical knowledge in teaching', 'she did not know how to recognise and develop possibilities for worthwhile academic learning'), of their situations (e.g. 'the classroom setting . . . did not offer the necessary structure for learning') or of those working with them (e.g. 'because [the supervising teacher] did not act as a teacher educator'). On this basis very insightful judgments are made about individual cases and a useful critique of existing teacher education practices is generated.

As a way of using research on student-teachers' learning to provide a critique of current teacher education practices, the approach used by Feiman-Nemser and Buchmann may justly be viewed as a model, although the danger of over-generalising from the experiences of a few students must always be guarded against. Many of us, however, might be less confident than these authors about asserting what tasks *must* be undertaken in initial teacher preparation, especially if our thinking has to take account of existing economic and political constraints. At the same time, we might want to understand the learning of beginning teachers more fully, putting greater emphasis on explanation, and less on judgment, of how and what they learn.

In sharp contrast is the approach used by Macleod (1977) in a study of student-teachers' learning in the context of a microteaching programme. The programme extended over the greater part of a semester and focused on three successive teaching skills defined in terms of an extended version of Flanders' (1970) FIAC system for analysing teaching. After each microteaching lesson and the videotape replay which immediately followed it, the student-teacher was asked to write down his or her various reactions to what had happened in the lesson, and these reactions were then content-analysed. The foci of the student-teachers' reactions were categorised (on a commonsense basis) into six major categories (personal; teacher/teaching; pupils/pupil behaviour; lesson; situation; other) and forty-five sub-categories. Evaluative ratings of foci and structural links between them were also coded, so that students' statements could be reconstructed in terms of researchers' categories. This system allowed Macleod to reach conclusions:

- about student-teachers' overall emphases in reacting to their teaching (e.g. that the teacher/teaching category consistently accounted for more foci than any other, but that only a small minority of these were directly related to the skills specified for practice);

- about trends during the programme (e.g. that personal foci reduced from relatively few to none, while pupils/pupil behaviour foci increased steadily, as did causal linkages between foci);
- about student-teachers' conceptions of successful teaching (e.g. that their evaluations of teacher and pupil behaviour and their perceptions of causal links between them tended to imply a different view of successful teaching than that of the skills exercise on which they were supposedly engaged);
- about relationships between reactions to one lesson and teaching behaviour in the next (e.g. that the predictability of teaching behaviour in one lesson from teaching behaviour in the previous lesson is considerably increased by taking account of reactions to that previous lesson).

Through these various kinds of conclusions, approaches such as this make possible new understandings of the process of learning to teach, understandings which are generalisable across substantial populations of students, following similar programmes in similar contexts. While not imposing a prescriptive framework, this kind of approach does, however, have the severe limitation that it does impose a standard system, applied in the same way to all student-teachers, not just on the interpretation of the evidence but on the evidence itself. Just as Feiman-Nemser and Buchmann's approach is especially appropriate for critique purposes, approaches such as Macleod's are most appropriate when generalisation is sought, although it would be greatly preferable to have a category system more firmly justified on theoretical or empirical grounds.

A third approach to gaining a more detailed understanding of the process of learning to teach and becoming a teacher may be exemplified by a study conducted by Zeichner and Tabachnick (1985; Zeichner, Tabachnick *and* Densmore, 1987). They saw themselves as within the same tradition as, for example, Lacey (1977) and as being concerned with the socialisation of teachers from a standpoint which emphasised the interactions of institutional factors with the concerns and capabilities of individual beginning teachers. They were concerned with the ways in which beginning teachers' *perspectives* developed during student teaching and during their first year of teaching, and with the individual, institutional and cultural influences upon the development of their perspectives. Following Becker et al (1961), they defined a perspective as 'a co-ordinated set of ideas and actions a person uses in dealing with some problematic situation'. and they emphasised the assumption 'that teacher behaviour and teacher thinking are inseperable and part of the same event'. The concern with problematic aspects of teaching, or 'dilemmas' (Berlak *and* Berlak, 1981) was also salient.

Thirteen student-teachers were selected from those following an elementary teaching programme in its final student-teaching semester, in order to obtain a group with diverse beliefs about teaching who were also doing their student teaching in diverse school settings. During the semester, each student was interviewed on several occasions about their beliefs and their experiences, whether their beliefs were changing and what was influencing them. Three of the interviews for each student-teacher were each based in part on a half-day's observation of her teaching and were concerned with the intentions underlying the teaching and the student-teacher's interpretations of her actions. Co-operating teachers and university supervisors were also interviewed about how the student-teachers' perspectives changed during the semester and about their influence on these changes. Four of these student-teachers were subsequently followed through their first year of teaching, with even more intense study of their thinking and practices at different stages during the year, and of the school contexts within which they were working.

The richness of the data collected by Zeichner and his colleagues enabled them, like Feiman-Nemser and Buchmann, to generate full rounded accounts of the thinking, the situations encountered, the strategies used, the problems faced, and the reactions to these problems, by each of the student-teachers and beginning teachers studied. Unlike Feiman-Nemser and Buchmann, however, they did not have a prescriptive model against which to compare these accounts; and unlike Macleod, they did not have a detailed predetermined system in terms of which the different accounts were to be coded. As a result they were free, and obliged, to understand each case-history in terms of the distinctive problems and opportunities with which the beginning teacher was confronted, and of the strategies she used to deal with them. They were, of course, also able, where appropriate, to draw on theoretical ideas from previous studies.

Faced with this task, they were able to derive important and interesting conclusions within the broad framework of their theoretical concerns. They were able, for example, to demonstrate the wide variety of perspectives adopted by the thirteen student-teachers and the unhelpfulness of grouping them into 'types', and to show that their student teaching did not generally lead to changes of perspectives but rather to the confirmation and elaboration of existing perspectives. They were able to show the variety of purposeful strategies adopted by student-teachers and beginning teachers, including 'strategic compliance' where severe constraints made behavioural conformity necessary but did not alter student-teachers' perspectives. And they were able to show that where beginning teachers attempted to impose their own perspectives on the teaching tasks they undertook, even when these perspectives were contrary to the policies and/or culture of their schools, success or failure depended upon a complex interaction of institutional characteristics with beginning teacher dispositions and abilities.

Zeichner and Tabachnick's work offers an excellent model for research on teacher socialisation, where the concern is to discover how beginning teachers' broad perspectives on their work develop, and how that development is influenced by different individual or institutional characteristics and concerns. There is a need for such research to be replicated and developed in a variety of contexts.

It is no criticism of such research, however, to suggest that it leaves unexamined many aspects of the process of learning to teach. As well as learning (or maintaining) broad perspectives, beginning teachers learn a great deal about detailed strategies and skills of teaching, about pupils and their behaviour, about learning and its assessment, and about being a teacher. All these kinds of learning are no doubt informed by the broad perspectives held by beginning teachers, and are also likely to inform these broad perspectives but they certainly cannot be taken for granted as part of the broad perspectives. We are therefore left with questions about the terms in which, and the means by which, the learning of the complex craft of teaching may best be studied.

Given our very limited knowledge about how the craft of teaching is learned, it would seem entirely appropriate that initial studies should make use of data-gathering procedures of the same open but intensive kind as those used by Zeichner and his colleagues, and also by Feinam-Nemser and Buchmann. But when confronted with such complex and voluminous data, which might easily seem 'ordinary' if looked at through the familiarising lenses of experienced teachers or teacher educators, we should be wise to be prepared with a repertoire of conceptual tools which might help us see such data with fresh scientific eyes. Some such useful tools might be derived from an understanding of what beginning teachers do generally and eventually learn, that is from a knowledge of characteristic features of the thinking and acting of *experienced* teachers. It is to a brief examination of what might usefully be borrowed from recent research in that area that the final section of this paper is devoted.

Differences between experienced teachers and beginners
There has been quite a dramatic increase in the last few years in research activity aimed at articulating the nature of experienced teachers' expertise. Some of the reasons for the development of research of this

kind were suggested by David Berliner in 1986 in his presidential address to the American Educational Research Association. Foremost among these reasons was that:

> the performance of experts, though not necessarily perfect, provides a place to start from when we instruct novices. The experts' performance provides us . . . with a temporary pedagogical theory, a temporary scaffolding from which novices may learn to be more expert. (Berliner, 1986, page 6)

The argument of this present paper, on the other hand, has been that our instruction of novices could be greatly improved if we understood the processes through which they learn to become experts, or at least to have the characteristics of experienced teachers. (Berliner rightly points out that although it is necessary to distinguish between experienced teachers and experts, it is also extremely difficult to do so in any systematic way.) The truth is that both research tasks need attention: in order to educate beginning teachers, we need to know what expert teaching involves *and* how people learn to become experts.

Our present need, however, is more modest: it is to identify some of the research conclusions about the characteristics of expert or experienced teaching, so that a knowledge of *what* kinds of expertise experienced teachers have learned may be used to help us investigate *how* such expertise is learned. The possibilities here may be exemplified by reference to four research areas or directions.

Planning
The considerable body of recent research on teacher planning is reviewed by Clark and Yinger (1987). One of their conclusions is that:

> the finer details of classroom teaching (e.g. specific verbal behaviour) are unpredictable and therefore not planned. Planning shapes the broad outlines of what is possible or likely to occur while teaching, and is used to manage transitions from one activity to another. But once interactive teaching begins, the teacher's plan moves to the background and interactive decision-making becomes more important. (page 95)

Correspondingly, as Clark and Yinger (1979) themselves found in a survey of teachers' planning practices, teachers concentrate on planning units of work or on weekly planning; only 7 per cent of their respondents mentioned lesson planning as one of the three most important kinds of planning for them. In contrast, student-teachers and beginning teachers are heavily dependent upon the detailed planning of lessons, as quickly becomes apparent when they attempt to do without such planning.

Experienced teachers would seem to have learned at least three kinds of knowledge and skill which allow them to dispense with planning the details of each lesson (although it can be argued that the best experienced teachers continue to plan individual lessons carefully).

First, many studies have documented the ways in which experienced teachers concentrate during the first weeks of the school year on establishing routine procedures and schedules for life in their classrooms. Such routines are of many kinds, relating for example to entering and leaving classrooms, distributing and storing materials, changing activities, and to different kinds of regular teaching/learning activities. Pupils are taught to follow routines with such thoroughness that for the rest of the year these routines serve as the frameworks within which the work of the class is conducted.

Second, experienced teachers do not generally need to work out analytically, or therefore to plan in writing, what they are going to do in particular lessons. Instead, a few written notes about important points may be used to complement 'lesson images', by which teachers can envisage the sequence of activities, the social organisation, the required materials and equipment, and pupils' likely responses. For any given curriculum, experienced teachers tend, on the basis of careful planning for the first two or three years, to build up a nested set of images of the units of work, and of the particular lessons within these, required for that curriculum.

Third, the capacity of experienced teachers to rely less on detailed planning than on interactive decision-making depends on their sophisticated skills, in recognising characteristic types of classroom situation (involving types of pupils, of activities, perhaps of content), and in responding to these situations with very nearly automatic choices of appropriate short-term goals to be attained and appropriate means for attaining these goals. Lacking such routinised decision-making skills, the beginning teacher is dependent on detailed advanced planning.

Ways of thinking
A second important area of research has been concerned with the contrasting ways in which experienced and beginning teachers perceive classrooms, select and use information, and make decisions. Much of this research has been with the use of specially devised laboratory tasks, but it has been only in recent years that such tasks have not tended to make inappropriate assumptions about the situations which confront teachers, and the ways they deal with them. Pioneer studies by, for example, Calderhead (1979, 1983) have been followed by major projects in the United States, notably that currently being directed by Berliner and

Carter (Berliner, 1986, 1987; Carter *et al*, 1987), although much of the work of this project has yet to be reported.

Research of this kind shows that experienced teachers are much more *selective* about the kinds of information to which they attend. For example, while student-teachers and beginners are generally keen to find out as much as possible about the individual pupils in a new class, experienced teachers are content to wait to meet the pupils, reassuring themselves only that these pupils are like others they have taught and attending to certain specific details, such as physical disabilities of any of the pupils. Experienced teachers are also less likely to accept information at its face value, but on one hand to *treat the perceptions of others sceptically* and on the other to *make inferences* from it in order to interpret and make sense of the situations or issues to which the information refers. Such interpretation involves assimilating new information to teachers' existing highly developed schemata, using relatively *abstract ways of categorising problems or possibilities.* Furthermore, experienced teachers' schemata tend not to be merely interpretive but rather to be *action-oriented*, related directly to the ways in which they know how to deal with things. Although experienced teachers are generally able *quickly to recognise types of situation* which beginners recognise only slowly or not at all, they tend to *take longer in initially appraising problem situations*, presumably because they know more about the information that should be looked for. Experienced teachers are generally prepared to *assert their individual ways* of interpreting and of acting, and less ready to accept pedagogical information or practices inherited from others.

Pedagogical content knowledge
Until recently, little theoretical or research attention has been given to the nature of the expertise involved in the teaching of particular subjects, although at a practical level this aspect of teaching has not been neglected in British teacher education programmes as it appears to have been in the United States. Increasing attention is now, however, being given to subject teaching expertise, most notably by Lee Shulman of Stanford University. Among components of 'the professional knowledge base of teaching', Shulman distinguishes 'pedagogical content knowledge' from knowledge of subject matter, from knowledge of the curriculum, and from general pedagogical knowledge (without, however, claiming any fundamental significance for these distinctions). He defines pedagogical content knowledge as follows:

> I still speak of content knowledge here, but of the particular form of content knowledge that embodies the aspect of content most germane to its teachability. Within the category of pedagogical content knowledge I include,

regularly taught topics in one's subject area, the most useful forms of representation of these ideas, the most powerful analogies, illustrations, examples,
explanations and demonstrations — in a word, the ways of representing and
formulating the subject that make it comprehensible to others. . . .
Pedagogical content knowledge also includes an understanding of what makes
the learning of specific topics easy or difficult: the conceptions are
preconceptions that students of different ages and backgrounds bring with
them to the learning of those most frequently taught topics and lessons.

(Shulman, 1986, page 9)

The Stanford studies on knowledge growth in teaching conducted
under Shulman's direction have been primarily concerned with the
content knowledge which people learn as they develop from being
graduates ('expert learners') in their subjects to become novice teachers
of these subjects. These exploratory studies themselves offer valuable
models for studying beginning teachers' learning and provide valuable
insights into that learning. Most usefully for present purposes, however,
they have developed a fuller empirically-grounded conception of
pedagogical content knowledge. Wilson, Shulman and Rickert (1987)
suggest that pedagogical reasoning begins with the teacher's own critical
understanding of the subject content to be taught, in terms of its
substantive and syntactic structures (Schwab, 1964): it is, however, the
transformation of that content for presentation to pupils that distinctively
requires pedagogical content knowledge. Transformation, they argue,
involves four sub-processes:

- *Critical interpretation* 'involves reviewing instructional materials in
  the light of one's own understanding of the subject matter;
- *Representation* involves the choice of metaphors, analogies,
  illustrations, activities, examples and assignments which will make
  the particular content most easily and satisfactorily comprehensible;
- *Adaptation* involves using one's knowledge of learners in general to
  modify one's representations so as to take account of likely mis-
  conceptions, difficulties, and other learner characteristics;
- *Tailoring* involves fine-tuning to take account of one's own particular
  pupils' characteristics.

It is not yet clear how experienced teachers differ from novices in their
engagement in such processes, or in the knowledge which they use in
them. What is clear, however, is that these processes require expertise
which beginning student-teachers have not developed but which is
essential for successful subject training.

Professional craft knowledge
Finally, recent research has begun to map out the nature of the

knowledge which experienced teachers use routinely in their day-to-day teaching. Brown and McIntyre (1988), for example, on the basis of phenomenological studies of the teaching of sixteen experienced teachers, concluded that common features of professional craft knowledge were:

- appraisal of the success of one's teaching in terms of the attainment of short-term goals conceived either in terms of *a normally desirable state of pupil activity* appropriate for the context and the pupils, or in terms of some type of *progress*, such as 'getting through the work' or the production of artefacts;
- teaching actions chosen from substantial repertoires available for attaining each of such kinds of goal;
- choice of appropriate teaching actions, and setting of appropriate standards for goal attainment, in terms of a large number of conditions relating to pupils, time, resources, content, and the teachers themselves.

Most striking about these consistent findings was the combination of the apparently automatic nature of most teacher actions with the complex conditionality of the actions chosen. The complexity of these conditional patterns of activity is especially impressive when compared with the insistent demands of many student-teachers for standard recipes for how to act.

Shortage of space has made it necessary for this final section to be both very summary and merely illustrative. The intention has been to indicate some of the concepts available from recent research on teaching which could be used as tools for examining the development of the thinking, knowledge and skills which beginning teachers use in their teaching. It is not, of course, imagined that student-teachers and beginning teachers would be found to show straightforward linear changes in relation to any of the concepts outlined. All that can be claimed — and it is a good deal — is that these concepts are relevant to the learning that sooner or later transforms the naive beginner into an experienced teacher; and, as such, these are concepts which should sensitise researchers to relevant aspects of such learners' teaching and thinking.

Conceptual tools such as these could therefore be used to study the finer grain of the processes of learning to teach and of how these processes complement the broader patterns of teachers' professional socialisation. They should not, in the first instance, be used to impose tight constraining frameworks for the collection and analysis of data, but should instead be used as an explicit repertoire available to researchers for interpreting relatively unstructured data, similar to that collected by Zeichner and Tabachnick. There is not only a need for new kinds of research, especially in the United Kingdom, into the processes by which people learn to teach: the means are available for such research to be done.

References

BECKER, H. GEER, B., HUGHES, E. *and* STRAUSS, A. (1961) *Boys in White.* Chicago: University of Chicago Press.

BERLAK, A. *and* BERLAK, H. (1981) *Dilemmas of Schooling: teaching and social change.* London: Methuen.

BERLINER, D. C. (1986) In pursuit of the expert pedagogue, *Educational Researcher*, September, 5-13.

BERLINER, D. C. (1987) Ways of thinking about students and classrooms by more and less experienced teachers. In: CALDERHEAD, J. (ed), *Exploring Teachers' Thinking.* London: Cassell.

BROWN, S. *and* MCINTYRE, D. (1988) The professional craft knowledge of teachers. In: GATHERER, W. A. (ed), *The Quality of Teaching.* A special issue of *Scottish Educational Review*, 39-47.

BUTCHER, H. J. (1965) The attitudes of student teachers to education, *British J. Soc. Clin. Psychol.*, 4, 17-24.

CALDERHEAD, J. (1979) Teachers' classroom decision-making: its relationship to teachers' perceptions of pupils and to classroom interaction. Unpublished PhD thesis. University of Stirling.

CALDERHEAD, J. (1983) *Research into Teachers' and Student Teachers' Cognitions: exploring the nature of classroom practice.* Paper presented at the American Educational Research Association, Montreal.

CARTER, K., SABERS, D., CUSHING, K., PINNEGAR, S. and BERLINER, D. C. (1987) Processing and using information about students: a study of expert, novice and postulant teachers, *Teacher and Teacher Education*, 3, 2, 147-158.

CLARK, C. M. *and* YINGER, R. J. (1979) *Three Studies of Teaching Planning.* Research Series, 55. East Lansing, MI: Institute for Research on Teaching, Michigan State University.

CLARK, C. M. *and* YINGER, R. J. (1987) Teaching planning. In: CALDERHEAD, J. (ed), *Exploring Teachers' Thinking.* London: Cassell.

FEIMAN-NEMSER, S. *and* BUCHMANN, M. (1985) Pitfalls of experience in teacher preparation, *Teachers College Record*, 87, 49-65.

FEIMAN-NEMSER, S. and BUCHMANN, M. (1987) When is student teaching teacher education? *Teaching and Teacher Education*, 3, 4, 255-273.

FLANDERS, N. A. (1970) *Analysing Teaching Behaviour.* Reading: Mass: Addison-Wesley.

FULLER, F. F. (1969) Concerns of teachers: a developmental conceptualisation, *American Educational Research Journal*, 6, 207-226.

FULLER, F. F. and BOWN, O. H. (1975) Becoming a teacher. In: RYAN, K. (ed), *Teacher Education* (Seventy-fourth Yearbook of the National Society for the Study of Education). Chicago: University of Chicago Press.

HOY, W. K. (1969) Pupil control ideology and organizational socialization, *School Review*, 77, 257-265.

LACEY, C. (1977) *The Socialisation of Teachers*. London: Methuen.

LORTIE, D. C. (1975) *Schoolteacher: a sociological study*. Chicago: University of Chicago Press.

MCARTHUR, J. (1981) *The first five years of teaching*. ERDC Report, 30. Canberra: Australian Government Publishing Service.

MACLEOD, G. (1977) Students' perceptions of their microteaching behaviour, Part 5. In: MCINTYRE, D., MACLEOD, G. *and* GRIFFITHS, R. (eds), *Investigations of Microteaching*. London: Croom Helm.

MORRISON, A. *and* MCINTYRE, D. (1967) Changes in opinions about education during the first year of teaching, *Brit. J. Soc. Clin. Psychol.*, 6, 161-3.

SCHWAB, J. J. (1964) The structures of the disciplines: meanings and significances. In: FORD, G. W. *and* PUGNOR, J. (eds), *The Structure of Knowledge and the Curriculum*. Chicago: Rand McNally.

SHIPMAN, M. D. (1967) Theory and practice in the education of teachers, *Educational Research*, 9, 208-212.

SHULMAN, L. S. (1986) Those who understand: knowledge growth in teaching, *Educational Researcher*, February, 4-14.

VEENMAN, S. (1984) Perceived problems of beginning teachers, *Review of Educational Research*, 54, 2, Summer, 143-178.

WEINSTEIN, C. A. (1988) Preservice teachers' expectations about the first year of teaching, *Teaching and Teacher Education*, 4, 1, 31-40.

WILSON, S. M., SHULMAN, L. S. *and* RICHERT, A. E. (1987) 150 different ways of knowing: representations of knowledge in teaching. In: CALDERHEAD, J. (ed), *Exploring Teachers' Thinking*. London: Cassell.

ZEICHNER, K. *and* TABACHNICK, B. R. (1985) The development of teacher perspectives: social strategies and institutional control in the socialisation of beginning teachers, *Journal of Education for Teaching*, 11, 1-25.

ZEICHNER, K., TABACHNICK, B. R. *and* DENSMORE, K. (1987) Individual, institutional and cultural influences on the development of teachers' craft knowledge. In: CALDERHEAD, J. (ed), *Exploring Teachers' Thinking*. London: Cassell.

12

Transitions and Early Education

Margaret M. Clark

Starting school

Age on entry

Foreigners could be forgiven for believing that children in Britain start school at five years of age and that this has not changed in recent years. Those in other countries reading official documents emanating from the United Kingdom may also gain the impression that this is likely to be true whatever the children's date of birth and wherever they live. What is true for England is often assumed also to be true for Scotland. This may be implied, erroneously stated, or the term Britain may be used where England is meant or should have been used. Research may have been conducted only in England and then overgeneralised either by the reader, or even the researcher, to include Scotland; the reverse is less likely! Vague and conflicting usage of the terms England and English Education does not help.

In England and Wales, children's entry to primary school is at the latest by the term after their fifth birthday. There are differences between local authorities, and even between schools within an authority, with regard to the number of entry dates per year, whether one, two or three. Furthermore, in authorities in England and Wales where there are two, or even three entry dates per year, children may be admitted as what is referred to as 'rising fives' (that is the term before their fifth birthday), or at over five years of age. A consequence of a policy of only one entry date, as is increasingly the pattern, is the presence in reception class of the complete age range from 4 to 5 years of age (otherwise the oldest children would not have gained admission by the required age).

'Four-year-olds in reception class' is currently one of the major topics of discussion in early education in England. Although it is indeed not a new phenomenon to have children under five years of age in reception class, the change of policy of a number of authorities to one entry date has resulted in many more younger four-year-olds being in reception class, including those who have just reached their fourth birthday. Concern is being expressed that resources may not be provided for the children admitted before the statutory age, that the adult/child ratio may be inadequate, that the curriculum may not be appropriate, and that this early admission may be adopted as a cheap alternative to preschool education.

In Scotland, where in contrast there is one entry date per year in all Regions, the age range on admission is also differently defined and the age range in reception classes is approximately 4 years 6 months to 5 years 6 months, the date of birth determining the precise age on entry for a particular child. Children are unlikely to be admitted as young as the youngest in reception class in England; the oldest children entering reception class in Scotland are also older than in England. It is possible for parents in Scotland to be appealing for their child's early admission, when a child in England of the same age might have been admitted to school as a normal consequence of an authority's policy.

An appreciation of these wide differences in age group in reception class between authorities in England and Wales with different entry policies, and of Scotland with a more homogeneous pattern and different age group, is important as it has implications for any discussion of transition, and the curriculum in reception class.

These wide differences and the changes resulting in younger children in some authorities being admitted to reception class also has important implications for preschool education, where, as a consequence, the staffs in nursery schools and classes may have much younger children in their care. Even where there is some flexibility as to the precise age at which a child does enter reception class there is often pressure from parents for their child's entry to primary school at the earliest opportunity. Teachers in primary schools may share, and even influence, the parents' views, considering that the sooner teaching of the basic skills commences the better. Some may regard preschool education as at best a socialising agency, and the play they see or believe takes place there as at best a preparation for the 'real work' of schooling. It is no more the case that the earlier a child enters school the better, than it is a justifiable assumption that play without adult direction, or a purpose seen by the child, is necessarily educative.

It is not a new phenomenon for some children to start primary school well before their fifth birthday, nor are regional differences something recent. Wide differences in age on entry to primary school were found in a national sample of children in England, Wales and Scotland even of children born in a single week, 5th to 11th April 1970. The differences would have been even wider had a complete age group been studied. Many children were in primary school before their fifth birthday, and there were wide regional differences (Osborn, Butler *and* Morris, 1984 and Osborn *and* Milbank, 1987). The percentage of children entering primary school before their fifth birthday, in England and Wales at least, has increased greatly in recent years. These changes, the variation across the country and for children with different dates of birth is discussed in detail in Clark (1988), based on statistical records and evidence from research.

From the above it may be seen that teachers of reception classes may have a wide or narrow age range of children depending on the number of entry dates, and may have children of very different ages in the class. In some authorities, even neighbouring schools may differ in this way. These teachers may now be concerned with much younger children than the age group for which they trained, or were within the experience of those who trained them. This is only one of the changes in early education. Another change is the percentage of children for whom entry to primary school is at least their first transition within the educational system.

Availability of preschool education

Entry to primary school was indeed the first experience of school for most children in the seventies, at the time of the Child Health and Education Study (CHES) of the national sample of children referred to earlier, (all of whom were born in 1970). For some children it was their first transition, as they had attended a playgroup a few sessions a week. In 1972 it was the government's stated intention that, by the 1980s, preschool education, on a full or part-time basis, would be available for all children of three or four years of age whose parents wished it for them on a full or part-time basis. There was no suggestion that the mandatory age for entry to school would be lowered for all children. Had that policy indeed been implemented, some of the children most in need might have entered reception class without such experience and been doubly disadvantaged as the majority of their contemporaries would enter with shared experiences on which to build, which the teachers might even come to assume, and friendships already established. As is well known, economic constraints yet again meant that the planned expansion of preschool education did not take place. Nursery schools and classes already established were often under threat, and were simultaneously under the research miscoscope as a consequence of the Nursery Research programme funded by DES, SED, DHSS, SSRC, and the Schools' Council in the mid-seventies, planned to gain evidence for the anticipated policy of expansion (see DES, 1975 and Clark, 1988 chapters 2 and 7).

There has been so much publicity given to the failure to implement the policy of expansion that it does not appear to be appreciated that there has indeed been a massive increase in the numbers of children who do attend a nursery class or school before they are admitted to reception class. Indeed, for a number of children, entry to reception class is their second transition, since prior to nursery school or class they may have attended a playgroup. This trend masks massive inequalities in types as well as amount of provision between and even within authorities; provision, and even choice, is available to some families, and there is no possibility of access for others. The statistical information is differently collected for England, Wales and Scotland, differently reported for nursery classes and schools from playgroups, day nurseries and childminders. This makes it difficult to make assessment of the precise situation and makes it possible for the statistics to be variously interpreted! A detailed discussion is to be found in Clark (1988) chapters 3 and 4.

There is clear evidence from the statistical records not only that many more children under five are now in primary school but also that a much higher percentage of children now attend a nursery school or class prior to entry. Others will have attended a playgroup for a few half days per week either before or instead, or a day nursery on a full-time basis and possibly from a very early age. A study of the returns from the various authorities and Regions shows clearly just how unequal provision is, and that alternative forms of provision are not necessarily available in areas where there are few nursery schools or classes or where entry to primary school is later and nearer to the mandatory starting age. From research on demand and uptake of available preschool provision, it is also clear that those in the most deprived sections of the community are those least likely to make use of the available provision, for a variety of complex reasons. Even in an area such as Lothian Region, which already by the seventies had a very high level of preschool provision this was true (see Haystead, Howarth *and* Strachan, 1980). As shown by Shinman in *A Chance for Every Child* there are parents whom she refers to as 'high alienation' who are isolated, possibly depressed, and who do not utilise available services which are voluntary, or use them with any regularity — even where they have expressed a wish for such a service to be provided (Shinman, 1981). There are other parents who make a conscious choice to keep their children at home until they start primary school, for child-centred reasons, as did some of those in my study of *Young Fluent Readers* (Clark, 1976). There would be fewer parents making such a choice if they found their child would thereby be the only one entering reception class without such experience.

For some children, reception class is a transfer within the same school, and with their close playmates. The building they may already know, they and their parents may already know the teachers, the written and unwritten rules. Their teachers will know each other, and possibly, though not always, information helpful to the child's continued development may be passed on informally. By five years of age, some young children may already be sophisticated in adjusting to changes of setting and relating to different adults, having spent time in a playgroup and nursery class. There have been several studies of transition into reception class. In these, however, the focus has been on children for whom this is a transfer and not a first experience outside the home. In the research by the National Foundation for Educational Research, *And So To School* (Cleave, Jowett *and* Bate, 1982) this was the case. For most of the children in the more recent study, *Starting School*, the transfer was from the same preschool setting (Barrett, 1986). In the study by the present author, some children who were observed in reception class had attended a nursery school or class, others had not (Clark, Barr *and* Dewhirst, 1984). Children were also observed in the preschool units where it was possible to study both language interaction and patterns of friendship which had already been established and which helped smooth the transition. The children who were most elusive in this study, as in any observational study, were those who even thus early in their school career already had changes of school, and or frequent absence.

Ethnic minorities

In the study by Clark and others referred to above (Clark *et al*, 1984), the focus was on children from ethnic minority backgrounds. For many of these children English was a second language, of which some had little understanding on entry to nursery class, or reception class. Five schools were selected for study with varying proportions of children from ethnic minority backgrounds. The schools were very different in size, in the age group of children referred to as 'reception', in the proportion of children from specific ethnic backgrounds and in the competence in English of the children on entry. In some of the schools, for most children, entry was a transfer from the school's nursery class. The widely contrasting patterns found in these schools in two authorities in the West Midlands are mirrored elsewhere. The changes in the population mean that some or many schools may have most of their intake from ethnic minorities. Even within a particular school there may be rapid shifts as a consequence of housing and other policies locally.

The ethnic constitution of some areas in Britain has changed dramatically in the last fifteen years; other areas have remained relatively unaffected. Although born in Britain, children may not be fluent in English, and their teachers may not understand their language. Cultural differences may present real barriers for the child in transition from home to school, particularly when combined with limited mutual understanding of each other's language between parents and teacher. Teachers in such schools are unlikely to find the frequently cited major studies of language in the home, by Tough (1977), Wells (1986) and Tizard *and* Hughes (1984) for example, relevant to the problems they face. There were in these three major studies no children from ethnic minority backgrounds or for whom English was a second language, partly because of the period during which the empirical work was undertaken. Such children where present in the area were few, and were excluded from the samples. The findings of these three studies and the related issues are discussed in Clark (1988) chapter 5, where it is noted that there is little evidence based on observational studies of children from ethnic minorities in their homes at the preschool stage.

Where these children do have an opportunity to attend preschool education, and thereby they and their parents can early establish a contact with the educational system this may give the children a 'heard start'. There may be time and opportunity for the adults to talk with, and play with the children, and explain the aims of early education to their parents. Even then, there is research evidence of limited understanding of or respect for current approaches to early education in some of these families. They may find it so different from what they experienced themselves or expect for their children. Some may define good education in terms only of a didactic presentation of basic skills, and rote learning as early as possible.

Children with special needs
The Warnock Report (1978) recommended that, where possible, children with special needs should attend normal preschools. It was not intended, however, that this should be by priority admission resulting in high numbers of such children in any particular nursery school or class. Rather it was hoped that this would be achieved by an increase in the availability of such provision. The present author undertook two studies of children with special needs in ordinary preschool units, one pre-Warnock in Scotland (Clark *and* Cheyne, 1979), the other post-Warnock in the West Midlands (Clark, Robson *and* Browning, 1982). There was evidence in both studies of a number of such children in ordinary preschool units, including day nurseries and, particularly in rural areas, in playgroups. Children with language difficulties, either alone or in association with other difficulties, were common among those with special needs. Some of the children were retained a further year in the preschool unit, in the hope that delaying their entry to primary school might increase their chances of a successful transition. Such children at the preschool stage were in units where the adult/child ratio might facilitate their communication. The availability of only one adult in the

reception class combined with the pressures to teach the basics to the other children made it more difficult both for the children with special needs and their teacher in the reception class. Where there are many children for whom English is a second language, the difficulties are increased, for both teacher and child. Furthermore, differential diagnosis is a problem in these circumstances. A child might or might not be fluent in his or her mother tongue. Knowledge of this should have an important bearing on the appropriate procedure for helping such a child, but the information may be difficult to acquire.

The fluctuations and changes in age on entry to reception class have important implications for mainstream education for children with special needs, who if they enter reception class at a much earlier age may have less chance of succeeding. Where many or most children on entry have had experience in a nursery school or class the child with special needs is less likely to adjust to the reception class unless he or she has had comparable prior experiences. Where there are high proportions of children for whom English is a second language in the reception class this also will influence the attention which can be devoted to the child with special needs. If both child and parents are also not competent in the language of instruction, the problems will be even greater.

Transition and the curriculum
Studies in preschool units and in reception classes have shown that a very different curriculum may be offered to children, even of the same age, depending on whether they happen to attend a preschool or a reception class. Studies of transition also show that for some children the primary school may provide a less stimulating and challenging experience than these same children had previously, and to which they were responding — making meaningful choices, concentrating for long periods, engaging in dialogue with adults and sustained co-operation with peers (see Cleave, Jowett *and* Bate, 1982 and Barrett, 1986). On the basis of short-term studies in the early seventies, topics which should have priority for research were identified and projects were funded within the Nursery Research Programme (DES, 1975). One such topic identified was 'continuity and progression in the educational experience of children between three and seven or eight years of age'. Organisational issues rather than the curriculum have been the focus in a number of researches on preschool education, such as co-ordination of services or co-operation between services. Studies within schools have tended to be short-term in funding and to consider only transition from preschool to reception class, rather than continuity in experiences over a longer time span. Indeed as was noted earlier, most children studied, even in the seventies when this

was less common, entered reception class as a transition from a preschool unit, rather than direct from home. Even for such children there is limited information on similarities and differences in the children's experiences at school and at home before entering school or outside school hours. Thus little is known about continuity in experience for particular children between preschool and primary school or between home and school. Furthermore, there are some children who consecutively, or even concurrently, before the age of five attend several preschool services, and possibly also a childminder, and have entered reception class. Little is known about the problems faced by young children in adjusting to several different settings, whose aims may not only be very different, but whose expectations of the children may actually be in conflict.

In a recent study of 'continuity in early education' funded by the Scottish Education Department, Watt and Flett consider the role of parents and highlight the important role they play in children's adjustment to the various transitions (Watt *and* Flett 1985). They stress that parents are in the best position to provide long-term continuity for their children, but that this presents real problems for the parents and the professionals. They stress the dangers of misunderstandings, that few links appear to be established even where a child may be attending more than one preschool unit. Although the importance of the home did tend to be stressed, they found that there were few attempts to relate the child's experiences at home to those at school. Where this did happen, it appeared to be as a result of interest on the part of the parents. Within early education not only do children have to face possible changing expectations, and even incompatibility, so also do the parents who may by one institution be expected to participate actively, by another to accept the institution as the authority and to display a passively accepting 'interest' and support.

It was a very general assumption in the early seventies, one still held by a number of teachers, that education is needed to make good the deficiencies of the home, particularly in language interaction — and that it does so. Observational studies in the home, and of the same children at home and at school, are beginning to challenge too ready an assumption of such contrasts (see Davie, Hutt *et al,* 1984 and Tizard *and* Hughes, 1984). Research in the seventies tended to be on preschool education in isolation, and at a time when it came under considerable threat from economic constraints. There were thus real dangers that evidence from observational studies would be used to justify intended cuts. There have been a few studies in which children observed at preschool have been followed into reception class, including a sample of the children from the longitudinal study of language by Wells and his co-workers in Bristol

(Wells, 1986); that by Clark on early education and children from ethnic minorities (Clark *et al,* 1984) and that by Barrett on children entering reception class who were also observed at home after entry to reception class (Barrett, 1986). That many young children, and their homes, have greater potential than is often appreciated is clear from these studies, as is the danger that too narrow a programme and formal testing of young children, may together confirm teachers in their belief in limited expectations of children. In more creative surroundings and challenging situations which make 'human sense' to the children, they may show a very much greater competence. There are examples of such settings in reception classes and beyond as well as in preschool units. The free play ethos, choice and better adult/child ratio in preschools have potential for development of the children's language, ability to concentrate, for collaboration between peers and as a foundation for literacy and numeracy. The importance of choice of activities, and the crucial role of the adults in determining how effective the setting is, particularly for the children most in need, is clear from studies in preschool units such as those by Hutt, Tyler, Hutt *and* Foy (1984) and Sylva, Roy *and* Painter (1980). These observational studies in preschool units have shown in many young children a readiness for sustained attention, and intellectually demanding tasks given these contexts, something not always appreciated by those who assume children learn only when and what is taught!

Continuity with extension
There are great dangers in the isolation of preschool units from each other and of these units from primary schools. There is much to be gained from sharing of knowledge on the curriculum between teachers working at the preschool stage and those in the primary schools. 'Enabling dialogue' between professionals is needed as much as between teachers and children. There are also new insights from research, including experimental studies relating to literacy, numeracy and children's cognitive development (see Donaldson, 1978 and Hughes, 1986 for example). In a chapter entitled 'Curriculum Matters' these issues are discussed in Clark (1988), which is a critical evaluation of research of relevance to the education of under fives.

'Continuity with extension' in early education, an expression used by Watt and Flett (1985), must, they claim, be based on an appreciation of the importance of the preschool years. This also includes an appreciation of the contribution of the home to children's development, both preschool and outside school. Transitions in early education require, they suggest, 'compatibility' without 'sameness' and 'stimulation' without 'shock' for children and their parents, between home and school and between the different institutions involved. This makes economic and educational sense, yet is a challenge to achieve, requiring as it does resources as well as curricular changes. Pre- and in-service training of teachers and other staff involved in early education would also require to take account of these new expectations if continuity in early education is to become a reality.

References

BARRETT, G. (1986) *Starting School: an evaluation of the experience.* Final report to the Assistant Masters and Mistresses Association.

CLARK, M. M. (1988) *Children Under Five: educational research and evidence.* London: Gordon and Breach Science Publishers.

CLARK, M. M. (1976) *Young Fluent Readers: what can they teach us?* London: Heinmann Educational Books.

CLARK, M. M. *and* CHEYNE, W. M. (eds). (1979) *Studies in Preschool Education.* London: Hodder and Stoughton for the Scottish Council for Research in Education.

CLARK, M. M., ROBSON, B. *and* BROWNING, M. (1982) *Preschool Education and Children with Special Needs.* Report of research funded by DES. Birmingham University: Educational Review.

CLARK, M. M., BARR, J. E. *and* DEWHIRST, W. (1984) *Early Education of Children with Communication Problems: particularly those from ethnic minorities.* Report of research funded by DES. Birmingham University: Educational Review Offset Publication No 3.

CLEAVE, S., JOWETT, S. *and* BATE, M. (1982) *And So to School: a study of continuity from preschool to infant school.* Windsor: NFER-Nelson.

DAVIE, C. E., HUTT, S. J., VINCENT, E. *and* MASON, M. (1984) *The Young Child at Home.* Windsor: NFER-Nelson.

DEPARTMENT OF EDUCATION AND SCIENCE (1975) *Preschool Education and Care: some topics requiring research and development projects.* London: DES.

DONALDSON, M. (1978) *Children's Minds.* Glasgow: Fontana Collins.

HAYSTEAD, J., HOWARTH, V. *and* STRACHAN, A. (1980) *Preschool Education and Care.* Sevenoaks: Hodder and Stoughton for Scottish Council for Research in Education.

HUGHES, M. (1986) *Children and Number: difficulties in learning mathematics.* Oxford: Blackwell.

HUTT, S. J., TYLER, S., HUTT, C. *and* FOY, H. (1984) *A Natural History of the Preschool.* Final report to DES prepared at University of Keele, unpublished.

OSBORN, A. F., BUTLER, N. R. *and* MORRIS, A. C. (1984) *The Social Life of Britain's Five-year-olds.* A report of the Child Health and Education Study. London: Routledge and Kegan Paul.

OSBORN, A. F. *and* MILBANK, J. E. (1987) *The Effects of Early Education.* A report from the Child Health and Education Study. Oxford: Oxford University Press.

SHINMAN, S. M. (1981) *A Chance for Every Child: access and response to preschool provision.* London: Tavistock.

SYLVA, K., ROY, C. *and* PAINTER, M. (1980) *Childwatching at Playgroup and Nursery School.* Oxford Preschool Research Project. London: Grant McIntyre.

TIZARD, B. *and* HUGHES, M. (1984) *Young Children Learning: talking and thinking at home and at school.* London: Fontana.

TOUGH, J. (1977) *The Development of Meaning: a study of children's use of language.* London: Allen and Unwin.

WARNOCK REPORT (1978) *Special Educational Needs: report of the Committee of Enquiry into the Education of Handicapped Children and Young People.* London: HMSO.

WATT, J. *and* FLETT, M. (1985) *Continuity in Early Education: the role of parents.* University of Aberdeen, Department of Education.

WELLS, G. (1986) *The Meaning Makers: children learning language and using language to learn.* New Hampshire: Heinemann Educational.

13

The Role of Research

Sally Brown

In Chapter 2 John Nisbet has set out a framework which facilitates my task
of providing an account of how the contributors to this book have perceived
the role of research in relation to educational transitions. One of the
important matters which John addressed was that of the demand for
'relevance' in research. Let me re-emphasise his statement that

> the definition of relevance has to be drawn widely, to ensure that important issues
> are not excluded from the agenda, to give alternative viewpoints fair
> consideration and even to awaken new expectations of what might be possible.

As a collection, these chapters have ensured that 'relevance' has acquired
that broad meaning. But individual authors have manifest the relevance of
research in different ways in their chapters. To explore that variation I shall
use two other organising concepts introduced by John. These relate to
functions of research as 'instrumental' or as 'enlightenment'.

The instrumental function of research

Here the concern is with research which has a direct contribution to
educational policy and practice. It is often referred to as 'practical research'
and, as John says, is designed for 'helping people to achieve what they . . .
want to achieve'. Its 'findings are readily incorporated into policy or action'
and so its impact is clearly evident. But, he argues, this kind of contribution
from research is possible *'only in non-controversial areas where there is
consensus on values'* (my emphasis).

This concept of the function of research seems to be what Gordon Kirk
has in mind when he draws attention to the enquiries which he sees as having
had a significant role. He cites the work which has been done in drawing
attention to the theory-practice gap in teacher-education, pointing to the
need for closer integration of college-based and placement-based activities,
and focusing on the fostering of partnerships to encourage a more prominent
place for teachers in the supervision and assessment of student teachers.
These matters are both of practical concern to teacher educators and, for the
time being at least, relatively non-controversial.

It is possible, of course, that an area which appears at one time to be non-controversial may change its status in that respect. John Nisbet's example of the shifting ground on questions about the 11-plus testing programme, is supplemented by Margaret Sutherland's account of research on gender differences at 11-plus. The demonstration by researchers that girls were apparently superior on verbal group tests of intelligence led to the manipulation of test results to ensure that 'boys would not be disadvantaged by what was assumed to be a temporary superiority of girls'. All the assumptions underlying that overt blatant act would now be seen as controversial, and anyone wishing to introduce such a procedure would be unlikely to commission research in support.

As a more direct example of the instrumental function Eric Drever's contribution appears to address matters which, for a large proportion of the educational community, might be seen as non-controversial. The advent of resource-based strategies, as a means of fostering individual-ised activities, is regarded by many as a possible way of dealing with the demands of mixed ability teaching and certification of pupils at a variety of different levels. Eric's research does not offer an immediate programme of work for implementation. It is much more a collection and analysis of data to enable the practitioner to understand resource-based strategies in a realistic and unbiased way. He disentangles the effects of such approaches and shows what realistically can be expected from them; this he contrasts with what is claimed for them. His challenge to the myths of both traditional and resource-based teaching is not a device to undermine the new ideas of pedagogy. On the contrary, he uncovers many of the positive results which could help persuade the sceptical to adopt a resource-based approach, as well as questioning some of the more ambitious goals of the resource-based enthusiasts. What is most important is that he has mapped out alternative courses of action which have, or could have, been taken. He has not told practitioners what decision they should take, but he has enabled them to understand the implications of making any particular choice.

Using a very different research approach, David Raffe's work has a similar potential to have a direct impact on policy and practice. One would have to recognise, however, that his area of concern, youth training, could not be claimed as entirely non-controversial. To the extent that policy-makers are committed to the effectiveness of such training, his analysis has findings to offer which should have a direct impact on decisions. He demonstrates the features of the evolving schemes which have tended to help in achieving the government's stated aims. But he also identified the profound barrier to such achievement which arises from employers' resistance to the development of YTS as a source of skills for the *external* labour market. That these findings reflect those of other studies of, for example, TVEI and adult and continuing education, makes them all the more powerful and confirms them as a sound basis for action. But will appropriate action be taken? Possibly not, and that is because this is not a truly non-controversial area. It is not hard to imagine resistance to David's statement that:

> If employers are sincere in asking the education and training system to produce a more competent, versatile and better prepared workforce, they must put their money where their mouths are: not only by providing more training themselves, but also by changing their recruitment and selection practices to favour the education and training programmes that attempt to respond to their needs.

Calls for more research are frequently justified on the basis of their instrumental function. Thus Margaret Clark's recommendations for research relevant to the early education of ethnic minority children and those with special educational needs, might be given considerable support because 'doing-our-best-for-those-who-might-be-disadvantaged' is apparently a non-controversial position. But the agenda of the policy-makers in power will determine which of the many possible research studies will be seen as candidates for funding, and John Nisbet gave us a powerful example of this in Chapter 2 by referring to the ways in which the 11-plus related research changed in focus over time.

Alastair Macbeth might also seem to be recommending studies which have an instrumental function in aiding decisions which relate to the place of parents in education. A closer examination of this area, however, shows that the focus of attention is by no means non-controversial. This does not deny the importance of the research he suggests, but it does suggest that if it were undertaken it might well not have a direct impact on policy and practice. For example, in calling for studies on home learning, Alastair appears to have assumed, like many of the rest of us, that 'equality of opportunity' in education was a fundamental aim. Nowadays, however, it seems that assumptions like that of an egalitarian kind are regarded by some policy-makers as simply relics of the '60s and '70s.

In a more sceptical vein, Donald McIntyre offers a warning about being too eager to make use of the instrumental function for research; 'the danger of over-generalising' from limited data is always with us. The impact of the vast array of research findings on beginning teachers he sees as of value in sensitising teacher educators to the broad perspectives of the process of learning to teach. But, he cautions, 'we should be wise to be prepared with a *repertoire* of conceptual tools' (my emphasis). While the impact of research of this kind may be seen as direct (on teacher educators), it is tempered by the knowledge 'that it leaves unexamined many aspects of the process of learning to teach'. He too looks to the future for the instrumental function: 'in order to educate beginning teachers, we need to know what expert teaching involves *and* how people learn to become experts'.

It seems that the various contributions to this book have thrown some light on the instrumental function of research. The idea that it reflects the impact of research in non-controversial areas has been helpful. But the analysis gets slippery because 'non-controversial' is so rarely an absolute term. Educational matters tend to be non-controversial within certain groups and, at any given time, only some of these groups represent a large proportion of society. Non-controversialness, furthermore, is rarely invariant over time.

Let us now turn to research which does not claim to focus on non-controversial areas or to have an immediate impact on policy and practice.

The enlightenment function of research

In contrast with the instrumental function, John Nisbet suggests that research for enlightenment generally relates to areas of education which are controversial. The influence of such research 'is indirect and longer-term, through analysis, new interpretations and new concepts accumulating over time to influence the climate of opinion — not so much offering solutions to problems but rather defining the problem to which solutions must be sought'.

Research of this kind often creates 'the context within which controversial issues are tackled . . . [and its] findings tend to be treated merely as if they came from one more pressure group'. Its enlightenment aspect, therefore, may well encounter or engender conflict, but its role is to advance new concepts or theories, change people's perceptions, question their assumptions, influence their aspirations and offer them new insights. All of these, John argues, are then 'gradually absorbed into popular discussion until they become a new climate of opinion'. Statements made by people in power become influenced without the speaker being at all aware of the research origins of the views expressed. Official documents incorporate, without acknowledgment, ideas which have emanated from research; for the documents' authors they have become just common sense, folklore or part of policy.

Examples of the unconscious absorption of research findings into everyday thinking and discourse are not hard to find. Assessment is an obvious instance. Today's public statements from politicians, teachers, examination board officials, HM Inspectorate and local authority officers, reflect very closely the ideas which researchers were articulating ten to fifteen years ago. Now these statements are seen as anodyne; previously they were regarded as highly controversial if not revolutionary.

In Gordon Kirk's chapter, he seems to be arguing that research has played no part in many aspects of the developments in teacher education with which he is concerned. His claim that, in terms of its influence on decision-making, research has to compete with 'the impact of pressure groups, political expediency, and perhaps even the power of charismatic personalities' is, of course, quite right. One must ask, however, to what extent has the thinking of these groups, politicians or personalities taken on board much that has its origins in research without realising that this was happening?

Several of the contributors illustrate, or call for, research which enlightens. As John Nisbet suggests, the findings of such research are likely to be 'readily taken up by those groups whose arguments are supported by the findings'. So, for example, Margaret Sutherland's request in Chapter 4 for research which will show 'whether educational policies and practices are changing, are having the intended effects or possibly producing some unforeseen and rather undesirable effects' is likely to be welcomed by those concerned about gender inequalities in education, but not by those responsible for its policies or set in its practices.

Chapters 5, 6 and 9 by David Hamilton, Ian Stronach and David Hartley, sit firmly in the enlightenment mould. There seems little doubt, however, that these contributions will be seen not as enlightenment, but rather as opposition, by a government responsible for the proposals for opting-out by schools from the local authority system and for a national curriculum (DH), for recent initiatives under the head of 'vocationalism' (IS) and for the push towards the curriculum developments which focus on pupils' social, personal and vocational skills (DH). Each of these three authors sets out to provide an alternative perspective on, or a new interpretation of, the various governmental initiatives. They provide substantial illustrations of the role of research to analyse or challenge current policies and practices, rather than simply to work within, and so stabilise, the frameworks provided by those in power. These challenges come, of course, in areas which are controversial; frequently it is the researchers themselves who reveal the controversiality.

Sometimes, however, research fulfils an enlightenment function by defining new problems, or offering new interpretations and ideas, in areas which might be called controversial in the sense that they have never been thoroughly explored, but are not necessarily a focus for conflict. Donald McIntyre exemplifies this in his account of research which sets out to understand the 'characteristic features of the thinking and action of experienced teachers'. As knowledge in this area builds up, we may well reach a point where it has a direct impact on teacher education, and so comes under the cloak of research with an instrumental function.

We might even find the same thing happening with a research on 'the micro politics of home-school relations' which Alastair Macbeth currently describes as a 'spicy topic to study'.

In conclusion

In this chapter, I have attempted to use the contrasts, introduced by John Nisbet, between instrumental research, which has a direct impact on policy and practice in non-controversial areas, and research for enlightenment, which has a longer term and indirect impact in controversial areas. These organising concepts have been useful in considering the different ways in which the other authors have dealt with research in their contributions. That is not to say, however, that each example of research can be unambiguously categorised as 'instrumental' or 'enlightening'. Some can be described only as enlightenment; but the instrumental examples seldom seem to be only that. Perhaps no area is truly non-controversial, and any study which has no new and challenging perspectives to offer cannot really call itself research. If research is about *extending* knowledge, then must it *always* have the enlightenment function whether or not it is also instrumental?

Before closing, I must return again to Chapter 2, which commented on the teacher-as-researcher movement and the trend towards the removal of the boundary between those who do research and those who use it. In Scotland, as elsewhere in the United Kingdom, there has been a growth of activity among teachers who wish to enquire into their own practice or experiences in school. Much has been made of the value of the reflection on practice which results from the teacher's sense of 'ownership' when he or she has the major responsibility for the research, with technical support from professional researchers. Yet none of the well-known researchers has chosen to take up (apart from passing remarks) this matter which was raised by John Nisbet. There are probably several reasons for this.

First, research of this kind tends to be highly personalised. In classroom action research, for example, a problem specific to the teacher is identified, theory is formulated, action is designed, implemented and tested, and the theory is then reviewed. If the understanding which is derived from the research is communicated to others (and often it is not), then it may be disseminated slowly through the profession, but only in so far as others find themselves in similar circumstances to the original teacher.

Secondly, as John Nisbet points out, there are dangers of initiatives of this kind forming a bandwagon, evangelising or trivialising research, being insufficiently analytical, critical or systematic. So far there is little in the way of reports from teachers' own research to confirm the reality of these dangers, but equally there is little to indicate a body of competent work.

Thirdly, it may be that the major transition theme, which we chose to ask the contributors to address, is simply not one which lends itself to extended discussion of teachers' own research. Certainly some of the authors have been extensively involved in helping teachers to carry out their own enquiries. Unless someone had chosen to take the changes in the boundary between professional researchers and the rest of the educational community as the transition focus of their contribution, however, perhaps we should not have expected a discussion of teacher-as-researcher.

Fourthly, while it may be highly desirable for teachers to adopt a reflective, questioning, research approach to their professional activities, we must remember that research and teaching are distinctively different. The sure-footed, extrovert, knowledgeable teacher who engenders confidence in pupils, pushes for successful outcomes and deals promptly with the myriad of situations which arise in the immediacy of the classroom, is *not* the same as the researcher who constantly challenges all his or her assumptions, systematically thinks through all the alternatives before taking action, and is just as interested in what can be learned from failure as from success. Because the individual cannot adopt both roles at the same time, the reflective research approach has to be accomplished outside teaching time. But teaching will always take most of the teacher's time, so research must be a more minor activity. Furthermore, there are some kinds of research which teachers may never have an interest in addressing.

And fifthly, although there is a great deal of rhetoric in support of the teacher as researcher, evidence of more tangible forms of support (particularly financial) is meagre. It has become much more difficult for teachers to undertake postgraduate degrees unless they can find their own fees. The tight budgeting of money and time in the colleges and universities has led to a dramatic decline in the help that their staffs previously gave generously and free to teachers. And SCRE, in trying to set up a Teacher Research Support Unit, has been given cheerful encouragement but, so far, very few promises of money.

All these reasons explain, to some extent, the paucity of teachers' research in this book. But the purpose of the volume was, after all, to celebrate professional researchers.